TUNDRA

TUNDRA

*Kolyma River*

*Indirika River*

*Lena River*

**CONIFEROUS FOREST**

*Angara River*

*Lake Baikal*

*Shilka River*

# THE SOVIET UNION

# THE SOVIET UNION

*By the Editors of Time-Life Books*

TIME-LIFE BOOKS · AMSTERDAM

A CHILD'S FIRST LIBRARY OF LEARNING
VOYAGE THROUGH THE UNIVERSE
MYSTERIES OF THE UNKNOWN
TIME-LIFE HISTORY OF THE WORLD
FITNESS, HEALTH & NUTRITION
HEALTHY HOME COOKING
UNDERSTANDING COMPUTERS
THE ENCHANTED WORLD
LIBRARY OF NATIONS
HOME REPAIR AND IMPROVEMENT
CLASSICS OF EXPLORATION
PLANET EARTH
PEOPLES OF THE WILD
THE EPIC OF FLIGHT
THE SEAFARERS
WORLD WAR II
THE GOOD COOK
THE TIME-LIFE ENCYCLOPAEDIA
OF GARDENING
THE GREAT CITIES
THE OLD WEST
THE WORLD'S WILD PLACES
LIFE LIBRARY OF PHOTOGRAPHY
TIME-LIFE LIBRARY OF ART
GREAT AGES OF MAN
LIFE SCIENCE LIBRARY
LIFE NATURE LIBRARY

## TIME-LIFE BOOKS

EUROPEAN EDITOR: Ellen Phillips
*Design Director:* Ed Skyner
*Director of Editorial Resources:* Gillian Moore
*Chief Sub-Editor:* Ilse Gray
*Assistant Design Director:* Mary Staples

## LIBRARY OF NATIONS

EDITOR: Martin Mann
*Deputy Editor:* Phyllis K. Wise
*Designer:* Raymond Ripper

Editorial Staff for *The Soviet Union*
*Associate Editors:* Dale M. Brown, Betsy Frankel, Anne
Horan, John Manners, David S. Thomson (text), Jane
Speicher Jordan (pictures)
*Staff Writer:* Thomas H. Flaherty Jr.
*Researchers:* Karin Kinney (principal), Scarlet Cheng,
Denise Li, Paula York-Soderlund
*Art Co-ordinator:* Anne B. Landry
*Assistant Designers:* Robert K. Herndon, Mary Staples
*Sub-Editor:* Sally Rowland
*Copy Co-ordinator:* Margery duMond
*Picture Co-ordinators:* Eric Godwin, Linda Lee
*Editorial Assistants:* Cathy A. Sharpe, Myrna E. Traylor

*Special Contributors:* The chapter texts were written by:
Oliver Allen, Ron Bailey, Donald Jackson, Bryce
Walker, Keith Wheeler and A. B. C. Whipple. *Other
Contributor:* Lydia Preston

EDITORIAL PRODUCTION FOR THE SERIES
*Chief:* Ellen Brush
*Traffic Co-ordinators:* Stephanie Lee, Jane Lillicrap
*Editorial Department:* Theresa John, Debra Lelliott,
Sylvia Osborne

Correspondents: Elisabeth Kraemer (Bonn); Margot
Hapgood, Dorothy Bacon (London); Miriam Hsia, Lucy
T. Voulgaris (New York); Maria Vincenza Aloisi,
Josephine du Brusle (Paris); Ann Natanson (Rome).
Valuable assistance was also provided by: Felix
Rosenthal (Moscow).

## CONSULTANT

Vadim Medish, Ph.D., Co-ordinator of
Russian Studies at the American University
in Washington D.C., grew up in the Soviet
Union. He is the author of numerous
publications on that country.

ISBN 0 7054 0841 8

TIME-LIFE is a trademark of Time Warner Inc. U.S.A.
D.L.TO:1847-1990

Cover: Pedestrians cross Leningrad's Palace
Square. In the background looms one of the
city's most familiar landmarks—the
colonnaded tower of the Admiralty building,
topped by a gilded spire.

The Soviet Union's official emblem is shown
on page 1, and the national flag on page 2.
Both are decorated with the hammer and
sickle, symbolizing the union of workers and
peasants, and the red star, a badge of the
Soviet state.

This volume is one in a series of books describing
countries of the world, their lands, peoples, histories,
economies and governments.

Revised 1990
*Revision Editor:* John Cottrell
*Sub-Editors:* Frances Willard, Tim Cooke
*Consultant:* Robert Service

# CONTENTS

**1**
**19**
The Aspiring Generation
34 Picture Essay: A Love of the Outdoors

**2**
**45**
An Immense and Rich Land
58 Picture Essay: Railway of Young Heroes

**3**
**67**
A Country of Countries
80 Picture Essay: Peoples at Work

**4**
**91**
A Long and Violent History
108 Picture Essay: The Living Church

**5**
**117**
Giants of Imagination
130 Picture Essay: A Blessed Couple

**6**
**137**
The Second Revolution

156 **Acknowledgements**
156 **Picture Credits**
157 **Bibliography**
158 **Index**

**Instantly recognizable as the symbol of Russia, St. Basil's Cathedral in Moscow is a combination of nine churches—the central structure surrounded**

by eight domed chapels, each honouring saints on whose days Ivan the Terrible won battles against the Tartars.

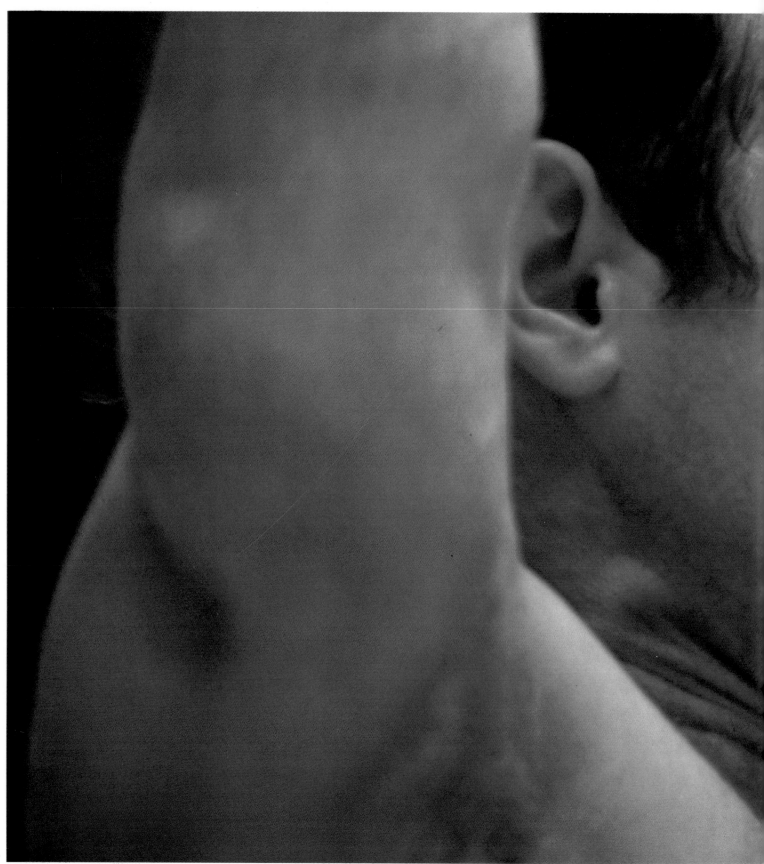

**Arms raised, a weightlifter grimaces during national competitions prior to the 1980 Olympic games. In the nine weightlifting events that year, Soviet**

# CHAMPIONS OF THE OLYMPICS

The glittering Olympic record of the Soviets indicates the national enthusiasm for sports of all kinds. Though it was not until the summer Olympics of 1952 that the Soviet Union entered the games, Soviet athletes won more silver and bronze medals than the United States. And in the winter Olympics of 1956, the U.S.S.R. gained the most medals and points.

Soviet athletics are supported by a complex of government organizations and based on a national fitness programme that attempts to include almost every citizen. The result is mass involvement in competitions. In one pre-Olympic contest, the Spartakiad, 55 million people took part in 27 events.

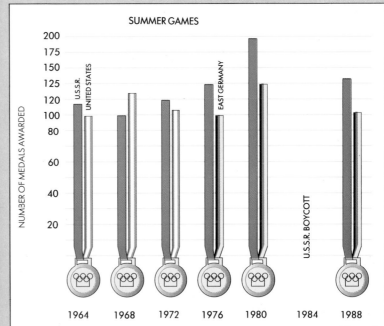

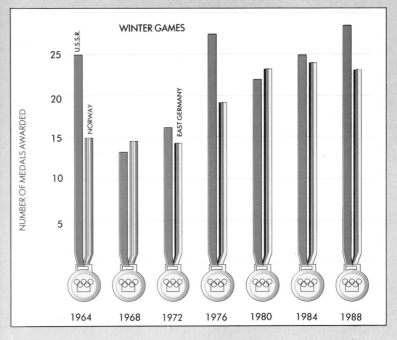

citizens took four gold medals—and athletes from U.S.S.R. satellites won the other five.

**Workers on a collective farm in Siberia sit down to lunch near their tractors, the widely used 130-horsepower DT-75M. Despite the harsh climate, the**

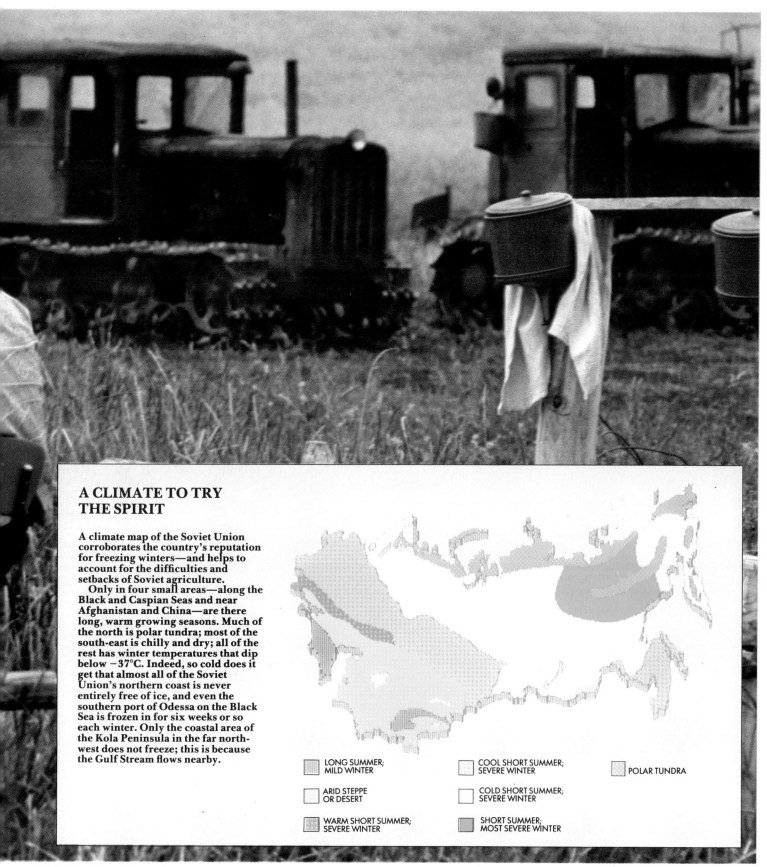

## A CLIMATE TO TRY THE SPIRIT

A climate map of the Soviet Union corroborates the country's reputation for freezing winters—and helps to account for the difficulties and setbacks of Soviet agriculture.

Only in four small areas—along the Black and Caspian Seas and near Afghanistan and China—are there long, warm growing seasons. Much of the north is polar tundra; most of the south-east is chilly and dry; all of the rest has winter temperatures that dip below −37°C. Indeed, so cold does it get that almost all of the Soviet Union's northern coast is never entirely free of ice, and even the southern port of Odessa on the Black Sea is frozen in for six weeks or so each winter. Only the coastal area of the Kola Peninsula in the far north-west does not freeze; this is because the Gulf Stream flows nearby.

LONG SUMMER;
MILD WINTER

ARID STEPPE
OR DESERT

WARM SHORT SUMMER;
SEVERE WINTER

COOL SHORT SUMMER;
SEVERE WINTER

COLD SHORT SUMMER;
SEVERE WINTER

SHORT SUMMER;
MOST SEVERE WINTER

POLAR TUNDRA

arable land cultivated in Soviet Asia has been almost doubled in the past two decades.

## WOULD-BE CONSUMERS

In the 1970s, as their government began to switch priorities from heavy industry to consumer production, Soviet citizens enjoyed an unprecedented rise in living standards. At the end of the decade, three quarters of all families owned a refrigerator and two thirds possessed a washing machine. Almost every home had a television set and 25 per cent of the sets were colour. Ordinary people's clothes were brighter and more fashionable than ever before. But the impetus could not be sustained. Restricted by an overcentralization, factories proved incapable of raising the quantity or quality of their output to meet the rising demand for consumer goods.

*Perestroika* (reconstruction), launched by Mikhail Gorbachev soon after he came to power in 1985, introduced a limited degree of private enterprise with the aim of correcting these inadequacies. But *perestroika* weakened the centralized economy without offering a radical alternative, and living standards continued their sharp decline. At the end of the 1980s, the gross domestic product per head of the Soviet Union was probably close to that of Portugal, the poorest West European nation. But low-quality goods and recurrent shortages made the plight of the Soviet consumer a good deal worse. By 1990, there was a chronic shortage of all major consumer items. Everywhere people queued for irregular supplies of such "luxuries" as cosmetics *(right)*, soap, washing powders, coffee, tea, sausages, sugar, butter, and even matches. In conditions akin to those of a wartime economy, shortages encouraged hoarding, panic buying, and black-marketeering. Sometimes they also necessitated rationing of such basics as sugar and milk. And while staples were cheap, other foods were very dear. In state shops, a poor-quality man's suit cost the equivalent of two months' salary, a pair of winter boots as much as a week's earnings. In the new privately owned co-operative shops, goods were usually less shoddy but several times more costly.

In Moscow's state-run GUM department store, shoppers crowd round the cosmetics counter to snap up the latest limited supply of products.

Customers must queue three times: to obtain a purchase note, to pay the cashier, and finally to receive their prize duly wrapped.

## ENTERING THE AUTOMOTIVE AGE

VEHICLES PRODUCED (IN THOUSANDS)

1,500

1,000

500

1970 1975 1980 1985 1990

Cars for personal use held low priority in the Soviet scheme until the late 1960s. Since then the output of passenger vehicles has quadrupled, far outstripping the modest increases in production of lorries and buses.

Even so, car-owning remains a luxury enjoyed by only 55 out of every 1,000 citizens. Annual running costs are more than a third of the average national income. Moreover, spare parts are scarce; accessories are so often stolen that many drivers automatically remove the windscreen wipers when parking their cars. And car use is largely limited to city areas where good roads exist.

Maintenance workers sweep leaves off the central reservation of a six-lane motorway, the Lenin Prospekt, one of the country's few modern roads.  The

U.S.S.R. has just 482,000 kilometres of paved roads—less than a tenth of the equivalent in the United States.

When they think of the Soviet Union, many people conjure up an image of a huge, cold country made up of lonely villages scattered amid dark forests and across open steppe and bleak tundra. The image is only partly accurate. There is no denying the size of the country. It is the largest in the world, with an area of 22.4 million square kilometres, covering approximately one sixth of the earth's land and extending over 11 time zones. And villages do indeed abound. However, the Soviet Union has become a predominantly urban society. Today, only about a quarter of its 289 million people still live in the countryside.

There are now over 2,000 cities and towns; around 15 more new towns mushroom into existence each year. Of the cities, 290 have a population of 100,000 or more, and at least 20 have a population of more than a million. Moscow, the 800-year-old capital that the Russians call simply "the centre", is the largest of these, with nine million inhabitants. Even far off in the Siberian wilds, Novosibirsk has a population of 1.4 million.

The growth of cities has been accompanied by a corresponding growth in their services. Moscow, Leningrad, Kiev, Kharkov, Baku, Yerevan, Tbilisi and Tashkent all have underground railway systems, and there are another eight cities that are scheduled to get them. Moscow's Metro, which is operated by a staff of 22,500, has 190 kilometres of track and 115 stations to serve about seven million passengers daily. The city's buses operate on 1,000 routes and provide passengers with 15 million rides a day.

Most of these people are housed in state-owned blocks of flats where rents are kept low (on average, about 3 per cent of family income). But the government has never been able to meet the need for housing, a problem which was exacerbated by the destruction of six million houses and apartment buildings during World War II. A post-war building programme continues unabated, providing two million newly constructed—though small—dwellings each year. In order to create new housing, 420 industrial plants turn out prefabricated sections, such as the one on the opposite page, which can be quickly assembled into buildings.

Meanwhile, as cities continue to expand, an effort is being made to regulate their growth, particularly that of Moscow, which has doubled its population since 1939. In 1975, 95 industrial plants were moved out of Moscow to reduce congestion and pollution. Current plans call for the diversion of heavy industry to 14 satellite communities that will be constructed around the city by the year 2000. A ring of parkland 48 kilometres wide is envisaged as a green buffer zone between the satellites and the city proper. Already 40 per cent of Moscow is made up of parks and public gardens, and on the outskirts is the so-called dacha zone of weekend cottages.

A prefabricated wall section, complete with windows, is hoisted into place during construction of an apartment building in Khabarovsk, in eastern Siberia. The same standardized parts are used in many regions of the Soviet Union to speed the completion of badly needed housing.

The urbanization of the Soviet Union parallels its conversion from an agricultural backwater to a major industrial power, a process that began under the tsars in the late 19th century and which has been pressed relentlessly since the Revolution. It has led both to remarkable achievement and terrible failure.

In 1917, the Bolsheviks took command of a country that was largely peasant and largely uneducated. Today the U.S.S.R. is primarily an industrial state, and universal literacy has been achieved under an educational system that provides compulsory schooling for everyone from the age of seven, and lasts at least eight years. The Soviet Union is the world's largest producer of oil and iron ore, its reserves of natural gas are in the region of 40 per cent of the world's total, its forests provide enough timber to make it the foremost producer of wood products, and it ranks only behind the United States and Japan in overall industrial output. It is a global superpower rivalled

only by the United States in military strength and in the exploration of space.

But the cost of this advance—in terms of human suffering and deprivation—has been staggering. Under Joseph Stalin, the Soviet Union's abrupt drive towards "modernization" involved a colossal demographic shift, with millions of people being transported in cattle trucks to forced labour in regions far away from their homes. Furthermore, his collectivizing of farms resulted in more than 10 million deaths and wiped out the *kulaks*— relatively prosperous peasants—as a class.

And Stalin's successors continued to expand industrial development with such disregard for the environment that, in 1989, a prominent Soviet scientist declared that 20 per cent of the citizens of the U.S.S.R.—some 57 million people—lived in "ecological disaster zones".

When the Soviet Union entered the 1990s, the excesses of so many repressive regimes had faded in the radiance of a younger, more enlightened leadership. But one pervasive legacy of Stalinism lingered on: a monolithic centralized institution, the Communist Party, which dominated political life throughout the multi-national, multi-ethnic Soviet empire and sustained an inefficient bureaucratic command system of managment that ruled the economics of the country and stifled the spirit of individual enterprise. The pressing need to dismantle this outdated structure represented the greatest challenge in the history of modern Russia.

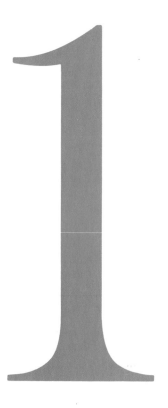

Primping while they watch strollers,
two young women relax on a Moscow
park bench on their weekend.

# THE ASPIRING GENERATION

In Moscow's Red Square, focus of Russian life since the Middle Ages, tourists from the far corners of the U.S.S.R. were engaged in a time-honoured ritual. They gazed up at the fantastic steeples and the asymmetrical onion-shaped domes of the 16th-century St. Basil's Cathedral. They walked beside the Kremlin's towering red-brick walls, where niches hold the ashes of Soviet heroes. They queued for over an hour to see the remarkably preserved body of Lenin enshrined in its red-granite and black-porphyry mausoleum.

It was a scene that could have been witnessed on almost any day since the end of World War II. But then hordes of sightseers left Red Square by way of the wide thoroughfare of Gorky Street, and instantly the sense of timelessness was lost. Above them flashed a huge neon Pepsi-Cola sign. Nearby, smart boutiques displayed the exclusive wares of Estée Lauder and Christian Dior. And at the junction with Pushkin Square, many of the tourists joined a queue even longer than that at Lenin's tomb—a queue for Moscow's newly opened McDonald's hamburger restaurant, the biggest in the world.

This was Moscow at the beginning of the 1990s, a time when the multi-racial empire of the Union of Soviet Socialist Republics was subjected to the most radical changes since, in 1700, Peter the Great, back from a fact-finding tour of Western Europe, embarked on a succession of sensational reforms designed to shake off the chains of outmoded Russian traditions.

In the late 1980s, another progressive Soviet leader, Mikhail Sergeyevich Gorbachev, had launched a crusade for economic and social reforms, eventually wielding his three-pronged pitchfork of *glasnost* (openness), *perestroika* (reconstruction) and *demokratizatsiya* (democratization). Now, so it seemed, the last decade of the century was witnessing the metamorphosis of the world's first Communist state.

For the first time since 1917, the 289 million inhabitants of the Soviet Union were being allowed freedom of expression and some real choice in elections. They were experiencing the freshness of a free press and almost totally open debate on economic and political issues on television. They were enjoying previously suppressed novels, plays and films. They were being introduced to free enterprise by way of privately owned, profit-sharing co-operatives that were allowed to compete with state projects.

In Moscow, especially, new signs of Western influence were everywhere in evidence. Citizens favoured America's best-known brand of cigarettes. Young people flocked to rock concerts. Calendars of Western companies now adorned every Soviet office. The magnificent old tsarist hotel, until recently named the Berlin to mark Soviet solidarity with East Germany, had reverted to being the Savoy. There was talk of building a five-star Hilton hotel not far from the Kremlin.

For the majority of Soviet citizens, however, glimpses of the Western way of life served only to raise expectations while increasing frustration. To be sure, many hundreds of Muscovites had enough roubles to take advantage of the opening of the McDonald's hamburger restaurant on January 31, 1990. But it qualified as a costly special treat, with the novelty of polite and guaranteed service at the end of the line. It had no bearing on the real, everyday life of the Soviet peoples.

That daily reality was to be encountered at Children's World, on Moscow's Dzerzhinsky Square. There, a woman from Volgograd, 900 kilometres to the south, waited in a long queue to buy a jigsaw puzzle. She had come in search of a tennis racket for her son, but to her dismay the country's largest, most celebrated toy shop had little more to offer than plastic dolls and ducks and a few cheap board games. In another queue, an out-of-town shopper explained that she was hoping to get a carpentry kit so that perhaps her husband could make the sledge she had sought in vain to buy.

The same scene was being acted out at GUM department store, one of Moscow's largest, four blocks south of Red Square. Here, back in the early 1980s, citizens were readily able to buy shaving cream from East Germany, toothpaste from Bulgaria, jumpers from Poland and dresses from Finland. But by the 1990s few items were imported from Eastern Europe. Customers had to settle for whatever happened to be available—mainly shoddy goods mass-produced by Soviet state enterprises. Clothing, furniture, pharmaceuticals, refrigerators, washing machines, all were in chronically short supply.

# 1

It was not entirely impossible to obtain modern consumer items. Many, for example, were on sale at Moscow's railwaymen's club, where the Soviet Customs were holding an auction of confiscated illegal imports. But the starting price of the cheapest lot—a Sony stereo tape-recorder—was set at 1,200 roubles, the equivalent of six months' wages for the average Soviet citizen. At the other end of the scale, two desk-top photocopiers sold for some 40,000 roubles—a sum the ordinary citizen would take more than 16 years to earn.

Infinitely more disturbing, however, were shortages of the most basic needs. All over the Soviet Union, citizens waited in long queues, sometimes for hours, to purchase such "luxuries" as soap, coffee, rice and matches. In many areas, milk and sugar were rationed. It was commonplace to hear shop assistants say sarcastically: "I'm sorry. I've nothing to offer you. We have *perestroika*, you know."

In fact, for the average Soviet citizen, the first consequences of *perestroika* were a fall in living standards from those of the early 1980s: the upheavals weakened the centralized economic system without setting full-blown capitalism in its place. The hardships were all the more acute because *glasnost* had begun to raise expectations. "There is more freedom now, but life is harder," said an elderly Moscow housewife. "It is fine to have *glasnost*, but it does not pay the food bills or buy a decent pair of shoes or gloves."

It was possible, however, to take a more long-term view. For example, a Moscow grandmother vividly recalled the living conditions of a family she knew in the 1940s—a near-illiterate husband, an overburdened and sickly wife, and 11 children. "All lived in one big, big room—in a barracks really" with several other families. "They had a curtain which they pulled across it, and they put the beds behind the curtain. They used to sleep in shifts."

But now, she went on, "the children are all grown up and married, and have their own children. Each has a flat. Small, only one or two rooms. But with conveniences—a stove, maybe a refrigerator. One even has a car."

In this longer view, a picture of relative progress emerges. Between the 1950s and the end of the 1980s, food consumption had doubled, from bare sustenance to 3,000 calories or more per person each day. The working week (by law, every citizen was entitled to a job) had shortened to an average

## RUSSIA'S CYRILLIC ALPHABET

The listing below of the Soviet Union's Cyrillic alphabet includes a guide to pronunciation and to the transliterations employed in this volume. The alphabet was named after Saint Cyril, a Greek missionary who helped convert ancient Russia to Christianity in the ninth century. It was originally derived from the Greek alphabet by Saint Cyril and his brother, Saint Methodius, also an early Christian missionary.

| CYRILLIC | TRANSLITERATION | PRONUNCIATION | CYRILLIC | TRANSLITERATION | PRONUNCIATION |
|---|---|---|---|---|---|
| А | a | as in father | Р | r | as in ravioli (rolled r) |
| Б | b | as in bit | С | s | as in Soviet |
| В | v | as in vote | Т | t | as in ten |
| Г | g | as in goat | У | u | as in pool |
| Д | d | as in dog | Ф | f | as in fit |
| Е | e | as in yes | Х | kh | as in Bach in German |
| Ё | e | as in yoke | Ц | ts | as in cats |
| Ж | zh | as in azure | Ч | ch | as in cheer |
| З | z | as in zero | Ш | sh | as in shop |
| И | i | as in machine | Щ | shch | as in cash cheque |
| Й | i | as in boy | Ъ | | hard sign, no pronunciation |
| К | k | as in kit | | | |
| Л | l | as in let | Ы | y | as in shrill |
| М | m | as in map | Ь | | soft sign, no pronunciation |
| Н | n | as in not | | | |
| О | o | as in note | Э | e | as in bed |
| П | p | as in pat | Ю | iu | as in cute |
| | | | Я | ya | as in yard |

of 41 hours, and day-to-day consumer spending had gone up threefold. Admittedly, only one of 15 families had a telephone, and only 55 out of every 1,000 citizens had a car. But almost all families now owned television sets and 25 per cent of them were colour.

Since the 1950s, real incomes had quadrupled. Meanwhile, such major expenses as housing and education were subsidized, so allowing people to save more than ever before. By the 1990s, the country was awash with paper money—an estimated 300 billion roubles in personal savings. But bank accounts paid interest of only 2 to 4 per cent and with supply falling hopelessly short of demand, there was precious little of value to buy.

This mixed picture of a basically secure life marred by serious and depressing failures in the economic system becomes clearer in close examination of individuals.

Three quarters of the Soviet people live west of the Ural Mountains in Europe, and 65 per cent of them are city-dwellers. Most of these urbanites are the children and grandchildren of peasants who left farm villages for such centres as Moscow, Leningrad, Kiev and Gorky in search of a better life.

For the offspring of peasants, the Revolution has paid off. Virtually all are literate, and some hold university degrees admitting them to a burgeoning middle class of doctors, teachers and engineers—the so-called intelligentsia, those who work with their heads rather than their hands. It is towards this group that the rewards of Soviet progress promise to flow most bounteously—and among whom the battle to secure them is most intense.

Founder members of this new class are Dmitri and Sofia Ivanov, who live in a 12-storey block of flats in the ancient Ukrainian city of Kiev. They share their flat with their son and daughter-in-law, who are saving for one of their own. Sofia's father was exiled to Siberia before the Revolution for being a Bolshevik, later becoming headmaster of a school there. Dmitri's father grew up in a tiny log house, its only amenity a wood-burning brick stove for baking bread and cooking the cabbage soup and potatoes that sustained the family. He volunteered for a Siberian "new lands" project in the 1930s, joined the party and later became the director of a dairy.

Like virtually all Soviet citizens. Dmitri and Sofia work for the government—he as a mechanical engineer for the railway, she as an art teacher at a Kiev high school. Dmitri earns nearly double the national average salary because his party membership ensures him a good position—while Sofia, their son and his wife between them receive more than as much again. The family's living costs are low because many necessities are subsidized by the state. They pay only 2 per cent of their monthly income in rent and party dues and income tax make no significant dent either. About a third of the family budget goes on groceries: although staples such as bread, milk and sugar are subsidized, meat and fresh vegetables are expensive because they are bought on the free farmers' market, where quality is better but prices reflect supply and demand.

The Ivanovs' flat, in a new section of Kiev, is one of millions built in recent decades. It offers unpretentious comfort: two small rooms for both living and sleeping, an eat-in kitchen, a hallway, a bathroom and a separate toilet cubicle. There is also a small balcony.

The Ivanovs have furnished the flat with an eye towards dual function. Sofas double as beds, a worktable becomes a dining table. The floors are bare, polished wood (rugs are uncommon) and one room displays a wall of books. The overall effect of the flat is similar to that of middle-class homes elsewhere in Eastern Europe. Scant personality emerges. ("When I die," complained one Soviet woman, "no one will know what kind of taste I had.

# 1

All my life I have bought what was available, not what I wanted.")

In the bathroom the Ivanovs have installed a washing machine; it cleans the laundry but does not rinse it or spin it dry. The water must be changed and each garment wrung out by hand, then hung to dry on the balcony. The hot water comes from the gas-fired heater that the Ivanovs bought; their building, like most, supplies only cold water.

Although the Ivanovs are proud of their apartment, they complain about its lack of space. Back in the 1920s the government decreed that each Soviet citizen was to be allotted 9.1 square metres of living quarters (excluding kitchen and bath), the equivalent of a room 3 metres square. But this goal has been reached in only a few of the large cities. Throughout the Stalin years, city-dwellers, such as the family described by the grandmother, crowded into subdivided communal flats which held as many as 60 people. A family of four was lucky to have a room to itself, while kitchen, bathroom and utilities had to be shared with other tenants. Even in Moscow and Leningrad, people still lived in wooden cottages with outdoor plumbing.

In the late 1950s, Nikita Khrushchev launched a massive building programme. Thousands upon thousands of five-storey blocks mushroomed. So hurriedly were the buildings put up that they began falling apart almost as soon as the mortar dried. On some, wire-mesh screens have been fitted like awnings to catch bricks that tumble down from façades above. People refer to these structures as *khrushchobi*, a derisive pun that joins the late premier's name with the word for "slum".

The *khrushchobi* are gradually being superseded by slab-like high-rise

blocks of nine to 12 storeys similar to the Ivanovs', assembled from prefabricated concrete panels and identical in design from Minsk to Moscow to Samarkand. Four out of five new structures are built in this way, reducing labour costs as much as 40 per cent and shortening construction time from two years to as little as three months.

Construction is less sloppy than in the 1950s, but new tenants may still find themselves varnishing floors, painting walls and installing utilities that the builders left unfinished.

A newly purchased puppy snuggles in its owner's fur coat while payment is made at the *ptichii rynok*, Moscow's thriving pet market.

Most of the new blocks of flats are grouped in satellite districts on city outskirts. Although the plans call for food markets and schools close by, this is not always the reality, and department stores and theatres—as well as the offices and factories where most residents work—are likely to be an hour or so away, by bus and underground.

Although the new flats go up at the rate of two million a year, the end is nowhere in sight. One fifth of all city-dwellers are still packed into the old communal flats, where they must argue over their share of the light bill and whose turn it is to cook dinner. And so a private apartment, even an unfinished one located on the edge of town, is a passionately sought goal for which competition is intense.

Nowhere is living space more desirable than in the Soviet capital. There is a saying that "Moscow is downhill from all the Russias"—the good things in life tend to flow there first. But before anyone can move to Moscow to share them, he or she must first obtain a residency permit. These permits are not easy to obtain: only a job or marriage to a Muscovite guarantees that the move will be permitted. Marriages of convenience may be contracted with Moscow residents who are total strangers. Vows are spoken, the place of residence is changed on the interior passport that everyone must carry, then money is passed under the table and there is a quick divorce.

But a residency permit is only half the battle. Nobel prize-winning physicist Pyotr Kapitsa told the story of how his cleaning woman managed to acquire her own flat during the Khrushchev era. Kapitsa, then working on a secret project, was given a direct telephone line from his home to Nikolai

Bulganin. Early one morning the cleaning woman lifted the receiver, roused Bulganin from sleep, and presented her problem. The next day the special telephone was removed but the cleaning woman got her flat.

High-level influence remains the best avenue to all such perquisites, but most people must use humbler means. One method is to join the street-corner bargaining at one of the city's unofficial housing exchanges. Here crowds of flat seekers mill about with placards announcing what they need and what they can swap for it. (Once a citizen obtains an apartment from government authorities, it becomes a small fiefdom that can be traded, rented or even bequeathed to children.)

In a typical exchange, a couple with a newlywed daughter offers to exchange a four-room flat for two separate units, one for each family. Also looking for a swap are a young painter and his wife trying to barter their two rooms for three in order to make room for their second child. As leverage, the painter has persuaded his parents to include their four-room flat in the deal. He wants to exchange his flat and his parents' for two three-room flats. Finally, after weeks of negotiation, an agreement is struck and six flats change hands in a deal involving eight families.

In part, because housing is so tight, urban families tend to be small among the ethnic Russians, who make up a bare majority of the population. Many couples limit themselves to a single child. Birth control pills are often difficult to obtain, but abortions are easily available (some women have undergone more than a dozen). As a result the birth rate among ethnic Russians is one of the world's lowest, about 16 births for every 1,000 individuals. To reverse the trend, the government imposes a 10 per cent income tax penalty on childless couples. Even so, those who choose to avoid parenthood come out ahead financially. Typically, the money they save is poured into their home.

One such childless couple are Anna and Volodya, two Moscow friends of an American exchange student and his wife. Anna is a handsome strawberry blonde in her late thirties who works as a supervisor in a paint factory. Volodya, her husband, is a tall, balding industrial technician in his forties, grown podgy from lack of exercise and too many boiled potatoes.

Anna and Volodya live in a three-roomed flat that they share with Volodya's grandmother, an ancient peasant woman with a merry, wrinkled face and a bun of thinning grey hair. The flat is furnished modestly except for a West German stereo, their proudest possession, which was purchased at great expense on the black market, along with a large collection of black-market records. Frank Sinatra and Ray Charles are the favourites.

As in most Russian families, the good life for Anna and Volodya begins at home and centres on the kitchen table. "Everything is better at home," says Volodya. "Stores are crowded, the metro and buses are jungles, restaurants are impossible to get into."

So it is around the kitchen table that couples like Anna and Volodya entertain. Food appears in no particular order, and family and friends jostle one another, elbow to elbow. Swept away by the intensities of Russian friendship, they linger on for hours, indulging in talk that runs from trivialities to cosmic issues of God and humanity.

Sometimes the meal is no more than a clear soup with some fragrant black

"Bruins Play Hockey" is the prize attraction of the Moscow Ice Circus, one of more than 80 troupes—with a total of 6,000 performers and 14,000 off-stage workers—that make up the Soviet national circus.

bread, or perhaps a mound of boiled potatoes and some pickled mushrooms—all washed down with glasses of sweet black tea or iced vodka. But at Anna's table, meals are more likely to take on another dimension.

Sunday lunch might begin with cabbage borscht or sorrel-and-kidney soup, followed by fresh tomatoes and cucumbers in soured cream, three kinds of bread, potatoes in butter, beef or duck swimming in gravy, then fried cheese cakes with home-made plum jam and a cream-filled gateau from a bakery. To drink, there may be wine from Georgia, cognac from Armenia or flavoured vodkas.

Maintaining this lifestyle requires unflagging effort from both Anna and Volodya. Like many people in other societies, they find that their regular pay-slips do not cover the comforts and luxuries they insist on having. "If you really get mad at another person," one Russian explains, "you put a curse on him: 'Let him live on his salary.' It's a terrible fate."

And so Volodya moonlights. He is a skilful photographer, and he has found an underground source for East German colour film, which is far better than Russian film. He uses it to photograph children, going round to the schools in Moscow and buying the principals' co-operation with bottles of Armenian cognac. Then he sells the photographs to the children's parents. "It's a very nice arrangement," he says. "The principal gets his cognac, the parents get pictures of their darlings that are much better than the black-and-white junk. And I, of course, make a profit."

Although freelance enterprises of this type are officially frowned on, millions of people engage in them. Such transactions are often the only way to obtain prized goods and services. Even a haircut is easier to get if the customer goes to the hairdresser's home, after hours, and pays extra to avoid the long waits at the government hairdresser's.

Among the chief practitioners of under-the-counter operations are salespeople in government stores, who hold back merchandise for special customers. The satirical magazine

*Krokodil* frequently lampoons this practice. In one issue it mimicked a store's public-address announcement of the arrival of new merchandise: "Dear customer, in the leather goods department a shipment of 500 imported women's purses has been received. Four hundred and fifty have been bought by employees of the store. Forty-nine have been ordered in advance by friends.

One purse is in the display window. We invite you to visit the leather department and buy this purse."

As the *Krokodil* satire indicates, this thriving underground trade depends more on favouritism than on outright bribery. People trade their own special advantages for those of others. Irina, the wife of a Leningrad musician who works for the Kirov ballet and opera, can always get tickets for a few of the seats set aside for high party officials and visiting dignitaries. Some she gives to a friend who is a surgeon at a large hospital, and in return the surgeon makes sure that Irina's family receives preferential treatment. The uneven quality of Soviet health care makes this good insurance.

Irina also passes on tickets to her hairdresser, or to a dressmaker who copies Paris styles from magazines that Irina borrows from her sister—who works for Intourist and gets Western periodicals. So Irina stays *à la mode* and the dressmaker goes to see the ballet.

This elaborate system of barter and favour-swapping is so pervasive partly because bureaucratic bumbling causes periodic shortages, partly because scarce imported goods are preferred over shoddy Soviet products. By the government's own admission, only 1.4 per cent of its consumer goods measure up to international standards. Factory-made clothes come unstitched after several wearings, and shoes are so poor that in a recent year one pair out of eight had to be rejected by the official shoe inspectors.

Mechanical products are notoriously unreliable. The country's best slide projector has to be turned off every 20 minutes to keep it from overheating. Even press studs do not always work. In a letter to the magazine *Krest'ianka*

# 1

*(Peasant Woman)*, one exasperated woman complained of buying "quality" studs that, while attractive, were nearly impossible to close. "I tried my hands, teeth, even a hammer—but nothing worked," she wrote. "Then I had a happy thought—pliers! Since then, I go nowhere without pliers."

Under-the-counter sales are also spurred by the inept distribution system, which causes sporadic shortages in mundane items. Months may go by when it is impossible to buy detergent, or toothpaste or frying pans. Once, in Alma-Ata, the shops ran out of ballpoint pens. One man recalls spending weeks looking for a broom; there were plenty of brush heads, he said, but none had handles. Yet a few months earlier the stores were carrying handles without the brushes.

Shopping can be a challenge not only because of shortages but also because of the way retail shops operate. To buy food for Anna and Volodya's Sunday lunch, Anna first must queue up to select the item—half a kilogram of cheese, for example—and determine its price. Then she must join another queue to pay a cashier and get a receipt. Finally, she queues up with her receipt, to pick up her purchase.

At each store she is shoved and jostled by other customers and is confronted by surly shop assistants. Soviet salespeople, who may be deeply warm and generous at home and with their friends, put on their rudest manners when dealing with the public.

Queuing is such a basic part of daily life that it becomes a job in itself. The average urban Soviet woman spends 14 hours a week queuing up—two hours each day. The Soviet press once reported that 30 billion woman-hours a year are spent in this manner.

Almost every time she leaves home, a Soviet woman carries with her a string bag, an *avos'ka*—for "just in case". Along her route, she looks for targets of opportunity. Whenever she sees a queue forming, she rushes to join it, often before knowing what is being offered. If the goods hold out and she keeps her place, she may be able to stuff her *avos'ka* with a woollen shawl or a pair of Italian shoes. More than likely she will also buy extra shawls or shoes, for relatives and friends. People know by heart the clothing sizes of brothers, sisters, parents and co-workers. In every factory and office, workers regularly slip away—despite periodic crackdowns—to prowl the neighbourhood in search of desirable buys, and to return laden with goods for distribution or resale to their fellows.

Men take on some of the shopping and queuing chores, but most of the burden falls on women. In their efforts to bring the good life home, women are the unsung heroines of Soviet society.

Housework, Lenin once remarked, is "barbarously unproductive, petty, nerve-racking, stultifying and crushing". This condemnation does not prevent modern Soviet males from leaving the job to women. The men neither cook, nor wash dishes, nor change nappies, nor mop the floor. When they arrive home from work, they simply settle down with the newspaper or in front of the television, and wait for their wives to cook dinner.

Although the men seldom help at home, most women help outside the home. They are the backbone of the Soviet economy, making up slightly more than half the work force. Some 65 or 70 million—about 85 per cent of all women between the ages of 16 and 54—hold regular jobs, the highest percentage in any industrialized nation. One third of the U.S.S.R.'s lower-court judges and 70 per cent of its doctors are women. There are more female engineers in the Soviet Union than in all the rest of the world.

On the 9 o'clock television news, a broadcaster reads dispatches from the United States against a background of Washington, D.C. The Russian words mean "Tass Reports", in reference to the principal Soviet news service.

Yet, even in the work force, women are second-class citizens, relegated to inferior positions. Many Soviet women who are called physicians or engineers have jobs that elsewhere are filled by technicians. The medical specialists, university professors and prestigious academy members are nearly all men.

As in other countries, most working women hold low-paying teaching and clerical jobs. While they receive the same pay as men for the same work, their average salary is a third less than that of men. But in Russia some even serve as manual labourers. Western visitors never fail to be astonished that Moscow's streets are cleaned by platoons of bubushkas with brooms, and that potholes are filled by women construction workers wielding picks and shovels. One Soviet joke calls women "not only the equal of men but also of tractors and bulldozers".

Of the 15 per cent of Russian women who do not hold down regular jobs, some are young mothers. Others are the privileged wives of scientists, athletes, military top brass and Communist Party élite. Still others belong to a shadowy fringe of avant-garde painters and poets who somehow manage to get by outside the official economy.

Rima is one such dropout. In her mid-thirties, half Georgian and one-quarter Jewish, she is a sometime poet who makes her way in the effervescent underground art world of Moscow.

Rima has a friend who holds exhibitions in her large flat, and Rima helps to set them up—preparing canapés, greeting guests, acting as a second hostess. Many guests are foreign diplomats and journalists anxious to meet Russian intellectuals, and Rima helps to smooth the way. A newly arrived cultural attaché may need language lessons, and she will arrange for them, or give them herself. She will also arrange for the black-market exchange of foreign currency for roubles, taking a small cut. Or she will earn a commission on the sale of a painting by an artist she is championing.

Rima's catch-as-catch-can income helps support two households. For the record, she lives with her parents in a large flat that also houses her daughter Natasha and her ex-husband Borya, an ill-paid translator with pretensions as a poet. "Of course I would prefer not to see Borya," she says, "but we Russians can't afford to be emotional that way." The housing shortage prevents Borya from moving out.

Each morning Rima cooks everyone's breakfast, dresses her daughter for school, cleans, shops for dinner, and then embarks on her frenzied round of cross-cultural dealings. In the evening she returns, cooks dinner, helps Natasha with her homework and perhaps washes Borya's shirts. Then she takes a 40-minute taxi ride across town to her second household. Rima's fiancé lives

Indulging a traditional penchant for hard drink, two Soviet citizens prepare to down a bottle of vodka in the street. The average adult drinks about 14 litres of spirits annually, more hard liquor than is consumed in any other country.

there, 19-year-old Vasya, another would-be poet who has dropped out of mainstream society.

Vasya shares a tiny ground-floor flat with several room-mates, and Rima prepares dinner for all of them—her second of the day. Her time with her husband-to-be is brief but intense, filled with jealousies brought on by Vasya's resentment of Rima's former husband. "What can I do?" she shrugs. "Vasya and Borya have talent, poor things; someone has to help them."

For Rima, staging parties and filling in as a hostess are paying jobs. For most Soviet women, entertaining at home is the main social activity—a generous spread of food and drink on the kitchen table like that laid on for Sunday lunch by Anna and Volodya. Most leisure time is spent at home, in company with friends and relatives, reading or watching television, although many attractions also draw people outside.

Reading is a national habit. In a country where literacy has increased from the pre-revolutionary 25 per cent to nearly 99 per cent, Soviet men spend almost an eighth of their free time over a book or newspaper, while women devote a sixth of theirs to this activity. The most popular book topics, as shown by a recent survey of library borrowings, are biography, travel, spy and adventure stories, and—to an astonishing degree—World War II. The memory of that struggle compels an anguished fascination.

Three daily newspapers—*Komsomol'skaya pravda (Young Communist League Truth)*, *Izvestiya (News)* and *Pravda (Truth)*—command readerships in excess of 10 million; a fourth, *Sovetskaya Rossiya (Soviet Russia)*, renowned for its conservative stance, has a circulation of nearly five million. In 1988, in the wake of *glasnost*, subscriptions to Soviet newspapers rose by 18 million, and often it became impossible to obtain the most popular papers and magazines without being a subscriber.

The demand for a wide range of weekly publications is no less great. Most remarkably, the public appetite for hard information has been reflected by the success of *Argumenty i fakty (Arguments and Facts)*, a crusading weekly newspaper that endeavours to provide authoritative answers to questions raised by readers' letters—more than 10,000 every week. In 1990, its circulation soared beyond 30 million.

Meanwhile, *Novy mir (New World)*, the most prestigious literary monthly, has achieved a huge circulation by leading the way in the publication of previously banned works, including Boris Pasternak's *Doctor Zhivago*, Vasily Grossman's *Life and Fate*, Anatoly Rybakov's *Children of the Arbat* and, most sensationally, in 1989, Alexander Solzhenitsyn's *The Gulag Archipelago*, a chronicle of the Soviet Union's once vast network of labour camps. In

addition to these Russian-language periodicals are numerous regional publications in local languages such as Ukrainian, Estonian and Tadzhik.

Then there is television. Men watch, on average, several hours a day, twice as much as women. There are four main channels, two beamed from Moscow to the hinterlands by satellite. Outlying districts have their own local stations. Programming varies. There is an educational channel, for instance, that emphasizes science. Sports, concerts, ballet and opera get saturation coverage on a special nationwide sports and cultural channel.

And there is the quintessentially Russian pastime of chess. The U.S.S.R. has some three million ranked chess players, including about 60 grand masters—nearly twice as many as Yugoslavia, the second most fervent chess-loving nation, and two thirds more than the United States. On summer evenings and weekends, countless devotees gather round permanent chess tables in city parks to play or cheer on local champions.

Away from home, an evening out may on special occasions—a wedding or anniversary—include a restaurant meal or a stage performance. But most often the excursion is to a cinema.

More than half of all cinemas in the world are in the Soviet Union; they sell about 40 million tickets a week, and tickets are cheap. Cinemas show some foreign films but mainly domestic productions. Some 150 features in several languages are produced annually in 40 studios in Moscow and elsewhere. Many are of very high quality—well acted, artistically staged and expertly photographed. The Communist regime early singled out film-making as an art form to be cultivated, and the

**A woman steps up to be weighed on one of the scales, tended by pensioners, that are a feature in parks.**

infuential work of prominent Russian directors of the 1920s—Sergei Eisenstein, Vsevolod Pudovkin and Alexander Dovzhenko—has been carried forward by modern film makers.

When not attending films, most people indulge a passion for sport and nature. Sports facilities—fields for football and volleyball, basketball courts, large indoor swimming pools—are provided by factories and municipalities. In winter, families go ice skating in city parks, and in winter or summer they head by car or *elektrichka*—electric commuter train—for the farmlands and forests that border the large cities. On such a *vykhodnoi*—going-out day—there may be picnics, mushroom hunting or cross-country skiing. For some, the destination is a dacha, literally a "country villa", although most dachas are not so grand. They tend to be little wooden cottages without water or electricity. Some are privately owned; others are government-dispensed rewards for special achievements. Often they can be rented by weekenders.

For the great majority who have no dachas, there are state-controlled resorts on the warm southern beaches of the Black Sea. Each summer the town of Sochi alone is host to some two million Soviet citizens who come there to take their holidays at government health spas on passes handed out by their unions.

Such passes entitle the recipient to a stay of three to five weeks, with almost 90 per cent of the bill paid by the employer. For this, the holidaymaker gets a bed, meals, mud baths, sunbathing and an organized routine. At one of these rest homes near Odessa, the daily schedule is: reveille at 7 a.m., half an hour of gymnastics before breakfast (served in two shifts), medical checkups and treatment, sports, an after-lunch siesta, cultural programmes, recommended readings and periods of sunbathing which are carefully monitored to prevent overexposure.

Most of the holidaymakers enjoy this routine. The major drawback to the employer-subsidized holiday is its separation of families. Husband and wife are often separated because they work for different employers. Consequently,

many families prefer to go south on their own and rent accommodation in the flat of a local resident. In most cities a government bureau helps visitors find lodgings, promoting a lucrative free-enterprise tourist trade.

Aside from this summertime fling in the sun, Soviet citizens find warmth all year round in the *bania*. Every hamlet and collective has one of these steam baths, where customers thrash their own—or each others'—sweating bodies with bundles of aromatic birch twigs to cleanse the dirt from their pores and the day's ills from their souls.

The most famous *bania* is Moscow's Sandunovsky baths, a lavishly ornate structure from tsarist times, with ancient, much-darned flowered carpets, lace-shaped lamps and moulding of plaster cupids. There is one bath for men and another for women, and a visit, which takes half a day, entails a well-established ritual.

A bather enters the dressing room and exchanges street clothes for a toga-like sheet, then walks into a steam room where the heat takes the breath away. In the women's bath birch-slapping is frowned on. But men flail away with the leafy bundles.

"Simply waving the birch switches caused the air to circulate and increased the heat and its penetration," wrote one foreign visitor of his experience in the baths. "We struck each other with the birches and pressed their hot wet leaves against our legs and arms and stomachs so that the heat burrowed beneath the skin and into the vitals. Sweat began to pour and soon the tips of my toes, the last to warm, felt the heat." There followed a plunge into a pool of icy water.

In the women's baths, the pool scene is one of unfettered freedom. "The

# 1

water around us was full of women playing tag, shrieking and ducking each other, paddling across the pool," reports a young American woman. "The pool itself was elegant, tiled in a mosaic design of garlands. In a niche at one end stood a gold statue of two cherubs, one attempting a half-nelson on the other. With their bulging bodies and home-made knitted bathing caps, the splashing women looked a little incongruous in this setting."

After the pool comes the scrubbing room where, on long marble slabs lined up like hospital beds, bodies are scoured with handfuls of fresh white-pine shavings until the skin is pink and tender. A quick rinse with buckets of cool water concludes the scrubbing, and the whole procedure begins again with another session in the inferno.

It is between bouts of steaming and scrubbing, however, that the main business of the *bania* takes place. Lounging in the panelled and upholstered dressing rooms, the regulars meet their friends. Here, over plates of dried salt fish (eaten to replace the salt lost through sweating) and glasses of ice-cold vodka or beer, they swap jokes and talk of their jobs and families, of troubles with boyfriends or girlfriends, of last night's football game or concert or the latest book. The *bania* is everyone's private club.

In the *bania*, at home around the kitchen table, at picnics or football games, the one constant ingredient of every social gathering is vodka. In the Muslim areas of Central Asia, religion forbids alcohol, but in the European Soviet Union and in Siberia every man drinks, and many women do too—in quantities that astonish Westerners.

The consumption of distilled spirits per adult citizen is 14 litres a year, the highest in the world. Vodka sales have risen fivefold since World War II. This covers only vodka made and sold under government supervision. It omits the illegal brew, *samogon*, distilled in large quantities in the countryside.

Contributing to this prodigious consumption is the Russian practice of gulping rather than sipping. Any festivity is punctuated by multiple toasts tossed back neat. Packaging adds to the problem; the vodka bottle is sealed by a metal foil strip but no stopper. Once opened, it will probably be emptied on the spot. Outside factories at closing time small groups of men often join in a rite called "three on a bottle". It takes about 10 minutes to empty a half-litre bottle.

Alcoholism is held to be the main cause of inefficiency at work, widespread absenteeism and an estimated two thirds of divorces, 70 per cent of all crime, and countless accidents. More than 50,000 men died of acute alcohol poisoning in 1980 alone—three times as many per capita as in neighbouring Finland, where alcohol consumption also runs high.

In 1985, almost immediately after he came to power, Gorbachev launched an all-out anti-alcohol campaign. It raised the legal drinking age from 18 to 21, limited hours when alcohol could be sold, and increased the price of vodka by a third. Two years later he claimed that his campaign was saving 300,000 lives a year. But by 1989, massive popular resistance had forced an easing of the crusade, and public drunkenness was rising steeply.

This rampant alcoholism is seen by many as symptomatic of a declining quality of Soviet life. But there is one element in their lives that offers the Soviet people hope: their children.

"We save the best for the children," they say. "They are our future."

For Elena, a language instructor at Moscow University, life's greatest pleasure is her two-year-old son, Sasha. Hour after hour she dandles him on her knee, cuddling, cooing and singing nursery rhymes, kissing him and stuffing him with sweets so that he stays plump. In winter, she swaddles him in layer upon layer of clothing—woollen tights, tunic, several oversized jumpers, scarves, felt boots, fur coat and hat—the bundling that turns Russian children, in one observer's eyes, into "walking cabbages".

Like most Soviet mothers, Elena will smother Sasha with love and protection almost up to his teens—feeding him too much, hovering over him as he plays and studies. "I want ten more like him," she says, although the housing shortage will probably limit her to Sasha and one other.

Pampered and spoiled, their every wish catered to, Soviet children are almost never punished or even scolded at home. Yet they grow up disciplined and obedient to authority. They are indoctrinated with the need to conform, to subjugate individual desires to the aims of the group, not only in school, but also in political organizations to which they belong—the Children of October for youngsters aged seven to nine and the Young Pioneers for those between 10 and 15. To be honoured for meeting the standards of the group is the highest commendation; to be humiliated for disgracing the group is the worst reprimand. And it is often the child's playmates and schoolmates—not parents or teachers—who apply this pressure for conformity.

The first lesson in conformity arrives as early as the age of three, when a child

A vase of flowers brightens a modest
Palace of Weddings as bride and
groom listen to the ceremony. A
Palace may hold 50 weddings on a
busy Saturday.

# THE SOCIALIST RITE OF MARRIAGE

In the secular Soviet Union, the
state makes a brave attempt to
endow weddings with official,
rather than religious, ceremony.
Legal registration of the marriage is
required, as in most countries, but
it usually takes place in a Palace of
Weddings *(left)* rather than a plain
government office. And it is
embroidered with time-honoured
customs: an exchange of rings, a
sermon on the commitment
marriage entails, and a nuptial kiss.
The state also encourages another
"socialist rite", a visit to a
monument or shrine *(left, below)*.

After these ceremonies,
traditional conviviality takes over.
A city-dwelling family may spend
six months' pay on a wedding
party. In the countryside, vodka-
fuelled celebrations may last three
days. The state even gives
encouragement to this feasting; the
parent can receive as much as 10
days' leave from work to prepare
for the festivities.

Following a recent custom, a bridal
doll is attached to the car used by the
wedding party. Brides prefer
traditional white gowns; grooms
usually wear dark business suits.

Newlyweds pose for obligatory
photographs with the town's patriotic
monument—here, a World War II
rocket launcher. In Moscow, many
couples leave flowers at Lenin's tomb.

# 1

may enter nursery school. Nearly half of all Soviet youngsters do. Some might already have spent two years in one of the state-run day-care centres set up to free mothers for jobs.

"The greatest offence a child can commit in kindergarten is to be different," observed an American journalist. From now on there is a right way and a wrong way to do anything, from eating to drawing a picture. "See how Mashenka holds her spoon," says a teacher to a child whose way with silverware is not acceptable. Or again, to a child who has drawn a large green flower with a little house under it: "Why don't you colour the flower red or yellow? You've seen red or yellow flowers. And the building must be taller than the flower. Did you ever see a flower bigger than a building?"

Each year the strictures intensify to press conformity on the group. At the age of seven a Soviet child starts elementary school, the girls dressed in black or brown frocks, the boys in blue jackets with shoulder tabs. For the next three years, from 8.30 to 2.30, six days a week, they learn basic courses by rote, with a heavy emphasis on mathematics and science. Written work must be executed in ink, and handwriting must conform to the accepted penmanship style and be done with the right hand; left-handedness is discouraged.

In school the children become members of "links" in a juvenile collective. Each member's standing depends on the standing of the link, so that all watch over the performance and behaviour of their fellows. Dr. Urie Bronfenbrenner, a Cornell University sociologist who has studied Soviet education, described how the link system works with the example of Vova, a boy brought before his link

Concerned that city children may grow up without knowing the sounds of the outdoors, biophysicist Boris Veprintsev (*left*) goes to the birch forest near Moscow to capture the sounds on tape. His recordings have sold more than a million copies.

because he is doing badly in mathematics. "What did you do yesterday when you got home from school?" the link members ask him. In reply Vova dodges their attempts to probe his efforts on mathematics.

"A month ago you were warned to work harder on your maths, and now you don't even mention it," insists the chairman of the link.

"I didn't have any maths homework last night," explains Vova.

"You should have studied anyway," they tell him.

When a classmate suggests that two link members should supervise Vova's home studies, he protests. "I don't need them. I can do it by myself."

"We have seen what you do by yourself," says the chairman. "Now we will work with you until you are ready to work alone."

Members of the link know the standing of each student because performance is graded constantly, on a scale of 1 to 5, in the student's daybook. "The daybook went up to the front of the room when a student answered a ques-

tion, and the teacher marked down a grade," explained the daughter of a Western journalist, who attended school in Moscow. "If a student got into trouble the teacher could ask for his daybook and write in a 2. At the bottom of each two facing pages, which represented a week, was a space for a weekly behaviour grade and a grade for the neatness of the assignments listed in the book."

Once a week the daybook goes home for a parent's signature. If it contains criticism of the child's behaviour, parents are expected to take responsibility for correcting it. Failure to do so can bring a summons from the teacher, or worse yet, the school may inform the parent's employers so that pressure now comes from the boss.

In the eighth year, an examination determines which children will continue general studies and go on to a university, and which ones will enter a technical or vocational school. Only one out of five students is actually accepted at a university.

The candidates are winnowed out by competitive examinations that are supposed to give all segments of Soviet society equal opportunities for advancement but in fact often fail to achieve this egalitarian ideal. For example, 50 per cent of the students entering the prestigious Moscow University are supposed to be the children of peasants and factory workers, but in reality the figure is closer to 15 per cent. The rest are the children of writers, musicians, actors, teachers and party functionaries—youngsters who usually have an advantage because they attend special secondary schools. In addition, most of the university's students are ethnic Russians. "One runs into an occasional Moldavian

Most Soviet children are treasured, even overprotected: this rosy-cheeked youngster is almost lost from sight inside blankets and furs.

or Kazak," says an observer, "but that is relatively rare."

Because a pass grade in the competitive examinations is a ticket to a better life, parents resort to various means, both legal and illegal, to help their children. Those who can afford it—as well as some who cannot—hire private tutors to coach their children out of school. The cashier in a Moscow cafeteria complained to an acquaintance that she and her husband were giving up their annual holiday. "We have to be able to hire a tutor for our oldest son so he'll have every chance to get into an institute," she said. Others use influence wherever it can be brought to bear, even passing a wad of roubles under the table to someone on the board of examiners. A few years ago the going rate for buying a pass grade was

reportedly 10,000 roubles.

When he reaches 18, every Soviet male owes his country two years of active military service—although for a university student this generally means taking officer reserve training to qualify as a junior lieutenant upon graduation. He then owes six months of service, which he can complete over the course of several summers. To repay the state for a university education, all graduates—male and female—are assigned jobs in their fields, often in remote Siberia, where the state is pushing development. Some, attracted by the pay and privileges granted for work on the frontier, settle there; but after the mandatory two-year stint, many look for jobs back in Moscow or Kiev or Leningrad, and pursue the good life.

Somewhere along this route, most

young people pause to get married. In more than half of all Soviet weddings, both bride and groom are under 20. The ceremony is usually performed in a state-run Wedding Palace, and has been quick and proletarian, although recent efforts have attempted to glorify it with extra ritual.

Traditionally, Moscow newlyweds visit Red Square to lay a wreath on the Tomb of the Unknown Soldier or to visit Lenin's tomb, and then hire a taxi or use a private car to ride into the Lenin hills to have their picture taken against a panorama of central Moscow. The taxi is bedecked with ribbons, and on its grille hangs a small token of their wish for children: a bridal doll for a girl, a teddy bear for a boy. "The children," well-wishers are likely to say, "they are our future."

# A LOVE OF THE OUTDOORS

Perhaps it is the very discomfort of the climate—mostly cold and windy for months on end—that makes the Soviet people delight in living outdoors. The national game, chess, is played out in the parks in all but the worst weather; boisterous family celebrations are likely to be in a rustic front-yard. Although many people live in towering apartments, on state farms as well as in cities, many others occupy individual, separate homes, each with a picket-fenced garden to bring within the family orbit the land loved so intensely.

Even the everyday chores of shopping, largely confined to the interiors of state shops, is more pleasant when it can be done out on the street, at stalls where farmers offer the freshest produce and meats, or at the corners where black marketeers sell scarce goods. But it is on holidays that the people of the Soviet Union can fully give in to their passion for the outdoors, carpeting beaches with their bodies, strolling through parks and sightseeing in the snow while the baby snuggles in a sledge *(page 42)*.

Chess players pass a warm afternoon surrounded by onlookers in Moscow's Gorky Park. Chess has been played in the Soviet Union at least since the 10th century.

At a dacha weekend retreat near Moscow, three generations celebrate a birthday with food, wine and guitar-accompanied song.

A mother leads her child past a single-family house, common in the countryside and villages. Most Russian couples today have only one offspring.

A block of new Moscow apartments, identical to those going up in many other cities, gleams behind a tenant's protectively wrapped car. The banner calls for worldwide Communist unity.

Despite a massive programme of housing construction (two million dwelling units built per year), a fifth of the urban population must, like these two women, double up. They and another woman share the use of the kitchen facilities.

# THE CHALLENGE OF SHOPPING

In her work break, a woman buys meat from an outdoor stand. Such stands are set up around Moscow by the state stores to alleviate crowding in the shops themselves. Vendors usually wear armbands to indicate the store they represent.

Shopping bags in hand, Muscovites line up outside a store, waiting their turn to buy high-quality shoes. Such queues form mainly for exceptional goods but may extend a block or more; one that existed for two days was made up of 10 to 15,000 people eager to buy carpets.

**Assistants in a state store tot up prices on abacuses. These simple calculating frames are also still commonly used in Soviet offices.**

Some of the 3.5 million holidaymakers who come annually to Sochi on the Black Sea, many as guests of their unions, crowd a black pebble beach.

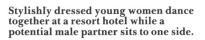

Stylishly dressed young women dance together at a resort hotel while a potential male partner sits to one side.

A study in concentration, warmly clad Moscow fishermen seated on the frozen river wait for tugs on their lines. They have used the augers (*above, right*) to drill holes through the thick ice.

A group of Soviet tourists who have brought along a baby in a wicker sledge admire the sights on a winter outing near Moscow. In the distance is the 13th-century monastery of Suzdal, which is now preserved as a national monument.

Strolling in one of the "park rings" encircling Moscow, a young family projects the new Soviet chic. On the bench sits a more traditionally dressed "babushka", or "grandmother".

A wan winter sun lights a snowy
stretch of the Soviet Union's Baltic
coast. From October to March,
Moscow receives on average 15
minutes' sunshine a day.

# AN IMMENSE AND RICH LAND

The most astounding feature of the Soviet Union is its size. Almost all of the United States, Canada and Mexico could fit comfortably within its borders. The U.S.S.R. is the largest political entity on earth, stretching 10,900 kilometres across two continents and through 11 time zones. Altogether, it spans a third of the Northern Hemisphere. To cross it takes seven days on the famous Trans–Siberian Railway (travellers making the trip come prepared with adequate supplies of beer and vodka, meat pies and cold fish, cheese and fruit). Leningrad is closer to Montreal, Canada than it is to Vladivostok, the Trans–Siberian's final stop in the east.

Lenin himself had the opportunity to experience some of this stupendous distance when he was sent into Siberian exile by a tsarist court. "Neither towns nor dwellings," he noted gloomily as his train rattled eastwards, "only a very few villages, and an occasional wood, but the rest all steppe ... for three whole days."

A popular patriotic song likens the Soviet citizen to a landlord proudly striding across his domain. And indeed he has reason for pride. That land contains an unequalled plenitude of the substances people covet: an estimated one fourth of the earth's energy reserves, a prospector's bonanza of minerals, seemingly endless forests and great tracts of fertile soil.

In its location on the globe, however, the U.S.S.R. is not nearly so fortunate. One third of it lies north of the temperate zone. (The offshore islands of Severnaya Zemlya are only 1,300 kilometres from the North Pole.) The interior is so far from the oceans that any ameliorating effect they might have on the climate is soon lost. As a result, the Soviet Union endures some of the worst winter weather in the world.

A close look at this immense land, from old Russia in the west to the Pacific coast in the east, reveals how nature has helped to shape the Soviet Union of today.

About a quarter of the country is in Europe; the rest sprawls across Asia, with the low-lying Ural Mountains forming the dividing line between the two. The Asian section alone is larger than the United States—Alaska and Hawaii included. The European portion, running more than 2,000 kilometres from the Barents Sea in the north to the Caspian Sea in the south, consists of a plain, through which four major rivers flow—the Volga, Don, Dnieper and Dniester. The longest of these, the Volga, empties into the Caspian, the world's largest inland sea.

If there is a single word to characterize the geography of the Soviet Union, *flat* is it. Three quarters of the land is less than 550 metres above sea level. The only tall mountains in the country are in the Caucasus range—which contains the highest peak in Europe, 5,642-metre-high Mount

## 2

**In a land with much snow but few hills for tobogganing, slides were once immensely popular. They were constructed of wood and stood 9 to 12 metres tall.**

Elbrus—and in the Pamir mountains of southern Central Asia, where Communism Peak rears to 7,495 metres.

The monotony of landscape is offset north to south by the variety of vegetation zones. Winding in a broad band across the Arctic is the tundra, a semidesert where only mosses, lichens and stunted shrubs grow. It occupies 15 per cent of the country's entire land mass. At its southern limits, still above the Arctic Circle, the tundra gradually gives way to a zone where trees grow in ever-increasing numbers until they form the taiga, the dark and silent realm of spruce, larch and pine.

The taiga is the largest of the several zones and covers most of Siberia, as well as a large chunk of European Soviet Union. Where the climate warms slightly, conifers cease to dominate and mixed forest takes over; this, in turn, surrenders to deciduous trees that thin out in their southern reaches, yielding to steppe grassland. Steppe encompasses most of the southern half of European Soviet Union and rolls eastwards deep into Siberia. At its southern edge, where precipitation is too low to support grass, patches of semidesert appear. In Soviet Central Asia—the bulge of land abutting Iran, Afghanistan and China—there are true deserts, as dry and bleak as any on earth.

Buried in this ground lies a prodigious wealth of minerals. The Soviet Union possesses one third of all the world's proven coal reserves and expects to find, when its geologists have finished probing, that it has two thirds. That would supply the country with energy for more than 7,000 years at current rates of consumption. In the meantime, the U.S.S.R. is already one of the world's top coal producers.

Geologists reckon Soviet oil reserves to be the world's largest. The Russians have known for nearly a century that they possess a lot of oil; fields in the Caucasus region were pumping half the global oil supply before World War I, and are still producing. More recently the Soviets began to tap the even richer fields of Siberia. One region is believed to contain 14 billion barrels, as much as lies under the North Sea.

During Stalin's time the oil was left more or less undisturbed and coal was burnt instead. Since then, the U.S.S.R. has become by far the world's greatest producer, pumping 12 million barrels a day—two and a half times Saudi Arabia's output—and accounting for almost 20 per cent of the entire world supply. Of this, nearly four million barrels a day are exported.

In keeping with the abundance of oil, the Soviet Union's reserves of natural gas are thought to be about 40 per cent of the earth's total, more than three and a half times those of the United States. One field near the Arctic Circle may represent the world's highest concentration in a single area. To exploit its gas and oil, the U.S.S.R. has been building pipelines at a feverish pace, including a gigantic one running across most of Siberia and all of European Soviet Union into Western Europe.

The forests that cover so much of the Soviet land are another major energy source, providing heat for many rural homes. Not surprisingly, the country is the world's foremost producer of wood products. It fells and dresses about 368 million cubic metres of timber every year, equal to the entire production of Canada and Europe. Marshy parts of forested areas offer another harvestable resource—peat. The U.S.S.R. contains 60 per cent of the world's peat reserves. Made up of decomposed vegetable matter, the peat is cut in blocks, dried and burnt as a low-grade fuel, mostly to generate electricity.

As if coal, oil, gas, wood and peat were not enough to satisfy energy needs for years to come, the U.S.S.R. also has been developing its nuclear energy potential; more than a dozen nuclear energy plants were in operation by the early 1980s. Nor is water power neglected. The country has an estimated 12 per cent of the world's hydroelectric sources. A single dam across the 1.5 kilometre-wide Volga at Volgograd spins 22 turbines that put out 11.5 billion kilowatt hours of electricity every year; it is one of the biggest hydroelectric plants in Europe.

This abundance of present and future energy can be put to work on half the world's store of iron ore, among other raw materials. The deposits of manganese, which is needed for alloys, are unmatched anywhere. And there is no lack of other minerals essential to modern technology: chromite, tungsten, titanium, molybdenum, nickel, cobalt, copper, lead, zinc, asbestos, mercury, antimony, silver, platinum, gold and diamonds. Indeed, the diamond and gold deposits in the U.S.S.R. are thought to be greater than those in South Africa. The blue kimberlite diamond mines in the far Siberian North yield 12 million carats a year.

Resources for agriculture are as important as those for industry. Here the wealth in some essentials is outweighed by deficiencies in others. Of fertile soil and moisture there is plenty, though not always where needed most. Of sunshine and warmth, however, there is generally too little.

The U.S.S.R. possesses around 220 million hectares of arable land, and most of it is seeded to one crop or another every year. By contrast, the United States has 40 million fewer hectares of cultivable land, and seeds only three fourths of that total. The Soviet Union cannot grow enough food to feed its own people, whereas the United States is able to supply not only itself but often other nations as well, including the U.S.S.R. Historically the Soviet Union has averaged one poor harvest out of every three; between 1979 and 1981, there were three disappointing harvests in a row.

Most Soviet agriculture is concentrated west of the Urals in Europe. This is the core of the nation, home to most of its people and locus of the government. Here lie three of the greatest of cities— Moscow, Leningrad and Kiev, centres of transport and industry. South and west of Moscow, trending northwards from the shores of the Black Sea and the Sea of Azov, in the Ukraine, the Crimea and Belorussia, spreads the soil so renowned for its fertility that its name in Russian, *chernozem*, meaning "black

## A WORLD LEADER IN MINERALS

The wealth of the Soviet Union's natural resources is indicated by this comparison of Soviet output of minerals and fossil fuels with that of its closest competitors. Although South Africa mines more gold, and China more coal, the U.S.S.R. leads the world in the production of iron ore and oil, and is the second-largest oil exporter (after Saudi Arabia), shipping nearly four million barrels a day to Eastern and Western Europe. It is also a major source of diamonds—mostly of industrial rather than gemstone quality.

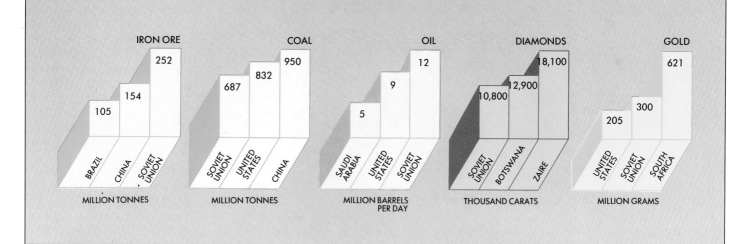

earth", is applied to similar soils in other countries.

Such fertility often fails because the growing season is frustratingly brief. It lasts only four to six months, compared with eight to nine months for Western Europe. The Gulf Stream, which does so much to warm Western Europe, brings little benefit to the Soviet heartland. What damp, warm air comes in from the north-west quickly cools as it moves across the plains. And the rains it brings fall all too often at the wrong time. Drought—or the opposite, too much moisture—plays havoc with the fields. Sometimes torrential storms strike when the grain is ripe and heavy, leaving the precious crop a soggy ruin.

Moisture for crops is a problem over much of the Soviet Union, even though the country gets about 13 per cent of the world's runoff of fresh water, the most generous allotment of any nation on earth. The trouble is that 65 per cent of the supply flows northwards, away from the agricultural regions and the warm but arid areas that might be made productive through irrigation. Two of the largest rivers in the European U.S.S.R., the Pechora and the Onega, and three of Siberia's, the Ob, the Yenisei and the Lena, spill their contents into the Arctic Ocean.

The Volga is the largest of the rivers that follow a southerly course, and it is the one most drastically redirected through a series of dams, primarily to furnish hydroelectric power for industry but also to irrigate farmland. A succession of 12 reservoirs impounds water with a total surface area of approximately 28,500 square kilometres.

By the 1970s, the Soviets had succeeded in irrigating more than one million hectares in the northern Caucasus and other sizeable areas in the south

West of Moscow, in Belorussia, a harvesting machine digs peat—partially decomposed vegetable matter, which is dried and burnt for fuel—from marshy land. Nearly half of the Soviet Union's peat is found in this region.

with water from the Volga. In the planning stage are irrigation projects that will double the total area under cultivation in this region. Rice is the principal crop in the newly watered land, which yields more than half the country's consumption of that grain.

This extensive tinkering with nature has had a price. The systems of locks and dams on the Volga and other rivers have slowed river traffic on these major transport routes and made the rafting of cut timber more difficult and expensive. Much worse in ultimate effect is the heavy loss of water through evaporation from the huge reservoirs that lie behind the dams. Along with the quantity drained off for agricultural and industrial uses, evaporation has sharply reduced the end flow into the great lakes to the south—the Aral and Caspian Seas. Both of them have been shrinking; the Caspian alone dropped 9 metres in 50 years.

In addition, wastes discharged by

upriver industries around Baku on the Caspian's south-western coast have polluted the downstream areas and taken a toll on fishing, once a major industry there. Especially hard hit has been the sturgeon, the great Caspian fish that can grow up to 4 metres long, weigh more than a tonne and live two to three hundred years. It provides the most renowned of delicacies, caviare.

The sturgeon swim up the Volga to lay their prized eggs. But as the river became increasingly polluted and more dams were built, fewer and fewer fish could complete the journey. The catch has decreased by half since the end of World War II.

Pollution controls subsequently cleaned up the water, and lifts made of wire were installed to raise the fish over the dams so that they could swim upriver to the spawning grounds. (The lift at Volgograd dam is designed to carry some 60,000 sturgeon in a season; it once stalled when 35 tonnes of the fish

**Framed by rocky outcrops, one of Armenia's ancient churches stands isolated on land now given over to cultivation. On the horizon can be seen the buildings of a state farm.**

crowded aboard at once.) Although these measures have halted the decline in spawning sturgeon, the production of caviare remains less than either the Soviet fishermen or the world's epicures would like.

Such drawbacks to irrigation schemes did not prevent the Soviets from considering plans for a far more ambitious project—nothing less than the reversal of the direction of flow of north-bound rivers. For at least 50 years, scientists have speculated about that monumental turnaround. The most recent idea, now apparently shelved, would have required 30 to 50 years to complete, and would have remade the land on both sides of the Urals. In European Soviet Union, three north-flowing rivers, the Onega,

the Northern Dvina and the Pechora, were to have been shifted into reverse, their flow diverted into the southbound Volga.

On the eastern side of the Urals, the Ob River—the fourth largest river in the world, known to Siberians as the grandmother of rivers—was to have been dammed just below its confluence with a branch called the Irtysh. Water from the enormous reservoir thus created would then have been channelled southwards to refresh the dying Aral Sea and to irrigate parched lands of Kazakhstan and Uzbekistan. At one stage, engineers contemplated carrying the water through a canal 1,450 kilometres long, to be dug in part by nuclear blasting, but protests from within and outside the Soviet Union

forced abandonment of that idea. Instead, the water was to move through ancient river beds that were discovered on satellite photographs and that coincide generally with a natural depression called the Turgay Trough.

If these grandiose proposals were ever carried out, they would constitute the most colossal engineering works undertaken by any people anywhere. They would displace thousands of Soviets, submerge ancient towns and hamlets, and impose ecological costs still beyond measuring, perhaps even altering the climate of the Northern Hemisphere.

The shelving of this scheme has produced disappointment for some. The Soviets have seen the effects of irrigation on 6.47 million hectares in the

# 2

southern regions of Kazakhstan and Turkmenistan in Soviet Central Asia. Herculean effort and an intricate system of dams, reservoirs and canals have made the sands bloom. In scattered artificial oases grow cotton, rice, tobacco, sugar beets, wheat and fruit. If the north-bound rivers were turned around to run the other way, another 60 million hectares could be seeded in this region.

To the obstacles nature has set in the way of farming must be added those arising from human action. The social and economic system of agriculture established by the Soviet regime has a profound effect on farm output, and some Western analysts hold the system largely to blame for the failure of the country to meet food requirements.

Stalin's first Five-Year Plan, inaugurated in 1928, called for total collectivization of agriculture under direct government control. The state seized ownership and operation of all farms, overriding violent resistance from many peasants, especially from the most productive and prosperous of them, the *kulaks*. Millions of *kulaks* were killed or arrested and sent to Siberia.

The state undertook to manage all aspects of agriculture from Moscow. Quotas for the production of various crops were set by headquarters; managers (some sent out for the job) were installed; harvests were sent to state-owned processing plants or to state markets for sale to consumers. Total state control proved too rigid, however, and after a few years it was loosened somewhat; all farm workers were allowed to cultivate private plots, producing whatever they wished to sell in free, competitive markets at prices higher than those of the state. This secondary system—largely government-run but allowing for some individual enterprise—has continued with only minor modifications since the 1930s.

Official figures document the lacklustre record of Soviet farming. Today, about 23 million people—a fifth of the working population—are engaged in agriculture. Comparisons with other countries are difficult because of the different ways statistics are compiled. In the United States, 3 per cent of the labour force works at farming, but this figure includes only those actually tilling the soil and excludes support workers—specialists such as mechanics who repair machinery. Some of the extra workers are counted as agricultural workers in the U.S.S.R.

Yet despite the incompatibility of statistics, certain measures do seem revealing. Soviet agriculture is heavily mechanized but it appears to be more labour-intensive than in Western countries. As nearly as can be worked out, 55 hours of labour are needed to bring 100 kilograms of beef to market in the U.S.S.R., 39 hours for pork. In the U.S. the equivalent numbers would be 3.1 hours and 1.3 hours. Of course, climate, as well as the Soviet system, must bear some of the blame for these and other shortfalls. Because winter lasts so long, livestock are kept indoors for at least two months more than in Western Europe. Feed that might otherwise be used to fatten grazing animals for the slaughter is thus spent maintaining them through the coldest months.

Where the influence of the system shows up most clearly, perhaps, is in comparisons of the productivity of

state-controlled agriculture versus that of the farmers' private plots. The individual plots are gardens of no more than half a hectare each. They account for just 3 per cent of the total area of land sown with crops, yet they yield 66 per cent of the potatoes grown in the Soviet Union and 33 per cent of the vegetables, meat and eggs.

Official agriculture, by contrast, is large in scale. There are two types of farms: collectives, called *kolkhozes*, and state farms, called *sovkhozes*.

The *kolkhozes* are like co-operatives; workers are paid in kind with a share of the crop and animal output. They are also paid a cash sum that is distributed after all expenses incurred by the collective are paid. The money is divided up according to the amount and type of work done, measured in "labour-day units". The state farms are "factories in the field", employing workers who draw straight salaries based on rates established by the government. The state farms also seem to be larger than the collectives (covering an average of 20,000 hectares, whereas the *kolkhozes* average only 6,000 hectares), but this

difference is deceptive: the areas with crops and the number of farm workers tilling the fields tend to be about the same on both types of farm.

The main emphasis in Soviet agriculture is specialization. Although the collectives raise a variety of produce and livestock, state farms tend to be more mechanized and to concentrate on a single commodity, such as grain or fruit. Specialization extends to the labour force on both types of farm: work groups are organized into brigades and are responsible for only one phase of the farm's operation, such as crop seeding or harvesting. Smaller teams, the *zven'ia*, are the lowest level of a work force on a farm and are, in many cases, headed by women. These teams usually concentrate on such specific chores as feeding pigs or milking cows.

The collectives are made up of family units, and membership in the *kolkhoz* is a birthright. One *kolkhoz* may include as many as several thousand families, but the average is 440. Generally the families live in villages near their fields, occupying cottages called *izbi*. The *izbi* lack indoor plumbing and central heat-

ing but have electricity. They possess a certain cluttered cosiness—lace curtains at the windows, windowsills overflowing with house plants, and possibly a draped icon in one corner. However, the *izbi* are gradually being replaced by concrete blocks of flats or individual houses equipped with modern amenities; some peasant villages now look much like Western suburbs.

On the state farms, particularly in the prosperous areas of Europe, workers generally live in flats similar to those provided for their counterparts in industry. They also get many of the services—good schools, day nurseries, cultural activities—that factories provide for employees. These perquisites make life on the state farms attractive to families. However, many young people, frustrated by isolation and loneliness and lacking any rights to the land, take advantage of opportunities to work elsewhere, and leave.

While the great state farms and big collectives of the black-earth country in Europe amount to a mechanized, mass-production food industry, the system of socialized agriculture in less

51

favoured areas can sometimes disintegrate, and both life and production can become grim indeed. In the late 1960s, a dissident Moscow writer, Andrei Amalrik, documented such a situation after he was banished to a struggling *kolkhoz* in Western Siberia.

The farm had been carved from the taiga, and in spring the *kolkhozniki* planted wheat, oats, corn, potatoes, clover and flax in the soggy earth. Flax and dairy products from 150 cows were supposed to be the money crops. But in Amalrik's first season of exile the flax harvest was a failure. Crews neglected to dry the seed so it could be made into linseed oil, and because there were insufficient people to card the flax stems for the linen mill, most of the crop was left to rot in the fields. The cows were supposed to be milked by machine, but frequently the machines broke down. Pipes intended to bring water to the barns were rusted out, and nobody bothered to replace them.

Most of the workers lived in tumble-down *izbi*. They quarrelled a lot. They swore a lot. And they drank a lot— home-brewed beer so potent that "three mugs were enough to knock a man out" or home-distilled vodka, made of rye rather than potatoes and "muddy green in colour".

Today, the rugged life on Amalrik's Siberian *kolkhoz* is perhaps less typical of that disproportionately large and mostly empty part of the Soviet Union than was the case in earlier times. Siberia is still a place to send prisoners and still a frontier, but it is also booming. Not only does the region produce 60 per cent of the nation's timber, but it also holds 60 per cent of the coal, the greatest share of valuable minerals, large quantities of rare and costly furs, and huge herds of reindeer that yield

**Proud in her snug cottage, a Ukrainian farm woman leans against a pillow-decked bed that doubles as a sofa. She has spread fresh grass on the floor and suspended boughs from the ceiling in observance of Pentecost.**

meat and milk, as well as leather.

One of the major problems implicit in Siberia's size is distance. The inescapable demands of moving people and things from one faraway place to another are extraordinarily difficult to meet in the ill-favoured terrain and savage weather. About a third of Siberia is almost entirely without road or railway. The only long-haul main road in Siberia takes off from the town of Never, a stop on the Trans–Siberian Railway 800 kilometres east of Lake Baikal, and heads straight north through the Stanovoy Mountains to Aldan, a gold-mining town, and on up to Yakutsk, about 1,100 kilometres.

With the uncovering of more and more of Siberia's riches, however, railway track is being pushed further into Asia. Where once the only steel track across the hinterland was the Trans–Siberian, there is now a growing network that reaches from Vladivostok nearly to Lake Baikal just above the Mongolian border, south to the city of Alma-Ata in the shadow of the Tien Shan range, and north to the outpost of Vorkuta in the Pechora Basin.

Improved transport is one indication of the rapid development of Siberia, particularly around Lake Baikal. The scimitar-shaped lake, 640 kilometres long and roughly 80 wide, is the world's most capacious fresh-water basin. It is also the deepest—a little more than 1.5 kilometres deep at one point. Formed 25 million years ago, it is home to 600 species of plants and twice as many kinds of animals, including some found nowhere else on earth, such as fresh-water seals.

Two cities stand on Baikal's shores. The smaller, Ulan Ude on the southeastern littoral, is the capital of the Buryat region. The other, Irkutsk, straddles Baikal's only outlet into the north-flowing Angara, which eventually joins the Yenisei and spills into the Kara Sea and Arctic Ocean. Before the coming of industry, neither settlement had an adverse effect on the lake, but now sewage and pollutants are jeopardizing the water's purity.

Irkutsk was founded in 1652 by rebellious Cossacks who came partly to get out from under the tsar's thumb, but even more to place the native huntsmen under theirs. The Cossacks were the first exploiters of Siberia's wealth, then believed to consist only of the splendid pelts of wild animals. Irkutsk became a major fur trading centre, and today it is probably the fur capital of the world. Its great warehouses are hung with pelts of white and silver fox, squirrel, ermine, mink, sable, polar bear, wildcat, otter and muskrat. In the old days, these animals were all taken by individual hunters; some still are, by private trappers licensed by the government. But now most kinds of fur animals, particularly silver fox and mink, are raised in cages. Like agriculture, the fur industry has come to be a collective enterprise.

The most highly prized furs are said to come from the Barguzin hills above Lake Baikal. The black Barguzin sable is honoured as the king of fur animals, and is still largely hunted in the wild. The animals do not reproduce easily in captivity. Even today some of the hunters follow their traplines through the snowy taiga on sledges drawn by reindeer; others, however, are ferried by helicopter. Purists go after the sable with dogs trained to use a "tender" mouth to avoid damaging the skin.

"When you follow a sable," said one hunter, "he can go anywhere—into trees, among rocks." The hunter dresses lightly because he runs all the time. He takes care to stay with his dogs, so that the sable will not burrow into the snow "before you can shoot him".

In the 1970s, the official income of the Soviet fur trade was more than £40 million a year. How much poachers earned from black-market sales cannot be estimated, but their profits were surely less than in the good old days of the fur trade in the 17th century, when a prime black fox pelt could bring its captor a cabin, 20 hectares of land, five horses, 40 head of cattle and a few dozen poultry.

When Irkutsk's principal industry was the fur trade, the city's inhabitants lived in log houses, their window and door frames and gables enhanced by elaborately cut mouldings. In the 1960s, many picturesque houses succumbed to the bulldozer as concrete-slab flats were built for 50,000 workers imported to convert the pristine Baikal into a gigantic power source. Two of the world's mightiest dams, the first at the Irkutsk outlet of the Angara River and the second downstream at Bratsk, were equipped with turbines to provide electricity for huge aluminium and wood-processing plants located on the shores of Lake Baikal.

It took 13 years to build the dams and the industrial complexes. Even before they were finished, they raised a storm of public outrage unheard of in the Soviet Union. Angry citizens, foreseeing pollution of the lake and destruction of the taiga, protested. "We are destroying our home," said Leonid Leonov, one of the Soviet Union's revered writers. "Baikal is not only a priceless basin of living water but also a part of our souls." One concern was the lake's unique crustaceans, the tiny epishura, which, by filtering 225,000

**Home from a successful hunt, a Siberian of the forested Altai region shakes out sable pelts while a companion examines fox skins. True sable is to be found only in the Soviet Union; approximately 100,000 pelts are sold each year.**

tonnes of calcium from the lake waters each year, guarantee its unparalleled clarity. Even Moscow listened, and equipment was installed to purify the industries' wastes. Despite these efforts, many ecologists remain pessimistic; a U.S.S.R. Academy of Sciences' report suggested that "the danger of Baikal being destroyed had increased rather than decreased," adding, "the entire lake was on the brink of irreversible changes."

Baikal lies at about lat. 57° N., and the lake by November wears a metre-thick covering of ice. At that point, the ice can be used for the transport of people and goods aboard lorries and sledges. Unhappily, the ice has a tendency to split into crevasses without warning. Many people in the area believe that the best way to travel on Baikal's ice is by horse and sledge, because if a crack suddenly opens, the animal will jump across it, pulling the sledge over the break.

However cold the Baikal area may be in winter, it seems semitropical compared with the region further north where gold, diamonds and oil lie; indeed, Irkutsk has come to be regarded as a favourite retirement city by workers living on the frozen northern frontier, where the temperature has been known to drop to below −67°C.

In this region, as in almost half of the Soviet Union, the surface is underlain by permanently frozen ground—permafrost. Occasionally, the permafrost exposes the remains of woolly mammoths, extinct relatives of the elephant, that were frozen whole in the ice during the last Ice Age; the stomach contents of one of these deep-frozen mammoths revealed that the animal had been browsing on buttercups just before its death.

In some regions the permafrost is 1.5 kilometres deep. During the brief northern summers, it may thaw to nearly 2 metres, turning the surface into a quagmire that can swallow lorries, tractors and other machines.

As an example of the destructive power of permafrost, Marina Gavrilova, a senior scientist at the Eternal Frost Institute in Yakutsk, told what happened to one of the first power dams

# 2

In a village near Irkutsk in Eastern Siberia, vendors sell milk frozen round wooden handles so that it can be carried home. Temperatures remain well below zero throughout Siberia during winter, but rise to as high as 37°C in summer.

built in this intensely cold area. "The engineers," she said, "were sure their hundreds of tonnes of concrete would withstand any stress of nature. An earthquake would probably not have hurt their dam, but its weight melted the frozen rocks underneath. The rocks crumbled and the dam split open."

In Yakutsk, as elsewhere in Siberia, buildings must be raised on stilts to allow the cold air to circulate underneath; otherwise, even the minimal heat seeping from their floors would thaw the top layer of permafrost and cause the structures to subside or tilt. Siberia is full of old structures that now lean in every direction; one traveller reported seeing a house that had sunk as far as its windowsills.

New construction techniques prevent such listing. In one method, the frozen ground is melted with a steam hose and 9-metre reinforced-concrete

piles are jackhammered into the muck, where they freeze fast forever.

Another trick is to use a pile containing pipes filled with paraffin (which will not freeze solid at the temperature of the frozen ground). To set the fluid-filled pile, the paraffin is heated so that the pile melts its own path down into the permafrost. Then the heat is turned off, allowing the ground to refreeze around the pile and clamp it tight. The paraffin is not pumped out but remains inside the pile.

Over the long winter, the paraffin is circulated by convection currents set up by temperature differences between ground level and the pile bottom, deep down. Because the ground is then colder near the surface than below, the paraffin at the bottom of the pile is warmer than the fluid near the top; it rises while the colder fluid falls, thus keeping all the fluid well-chilled. In

summer, this circulation stops, but the season of warm surface temperatures is so short, and the paraffin has been chilled to such a low temperature during the winter, that the fluid keeps the ground around the pile frozen at all times—and the pile is held firmly anchored summer and winter.

Winter is a cruel king. "In Siberia," goes a saying, "forty degrees below zero is not a frost, a hundred kilometres is not a distance, half a litre of vodka is not a drink and forty years is not a woman." Tyres burst from the cold, steel shatters like ice and rivers freeze to a depth of 6 metres.

Yet some labourers manage to work outdoors in midwinter; mortar is heated so brick can be laid in the freezing air. "The cold," wrote a visitor to Yakutsk, "makes the newcomer aware of his nose for the first time; every hair inside freezes rigid in a second. You can actually feel them bending with each intake of breath. Naturally you can see your breath, but what is more extraordinary, you can hear it turn to ice." One effect of this phenomenon is the "people mist", a sort of luminescent smog that is produced over Yakutsk by the moist emanations of human bodies and the exhaust of motor vehicles. Engines are kept running 24 hours a day to prevent them from freezing solid, and windscreens are double-glazed against the severe frost.

Schools are not closed unless the temperature sinks below −50°C. In homes, people live behind thick walls with triple storm doors and windows three panes thick. Women wear three to six layers of wool tights, and men pile on garments; no one carries metal coins in trouser pockets. Leather would freeze and crack within minutes, so everybody wears felt or reindeer-fur

**Offering a view of a wintry landscape, this window in a Siberian home is shielded by a sheet of glass with cotton batting stuffed between to block draughts. Unlike most, the window does not open; usually a small pane is hinged for ventilation.**

boots and carries shoes for indoor wear.

Drinking water is delivered to the home in solid chunks sawed out of the river, or is channelled through aboveground pipes that must be heated every few metres to keep their contents flowing. Milk is sold in brick form, with wooden handles inserted so that it can be carried home easily. Food is stored in bags hung outside windows, where it freezes and can be used when needed. A favourite delicacy is raw, frozen fish, served in crystalline pieces with suet, mustard or other accompaniments. A visitor who tried it found the slices without much taste, "but it was amusing to crunch them like sweets".

This is the land of the "long rouble", where workers are paid extra for services performed in bitter weather. The long rouble varies with climate and distance but follows a typical scale: 40 per cent above the going rate elsewhere just for taking the job, another 10 per cent after six months, double salary or even more for those who stick it out for five years, annual holidays of 42 days and, every other year, a return-trip ticket to anywhere in the U.S.S.R.

Long-rouble country is also known as young people's country; the average age of Sibiryaks—transplants from Mother Russia—is 29. The rugged environment and distance from civilization do no prevent them from leading an active social and cultural life. There are films, theatre, ballet practically as elegant as in Moscow, symphony orchestras, nightclubs and television beamed in from Moscow by satellite. The cost of making Siberia liveable as well as productive is high, but the potential return is higher yet. In the biggest land on earth, the biggest region—recalcitrant though it may be—holds inestimable promise.

# RAILWAY OF YOUNG HEROES

"The construction project of the century" is what the U.S.S.R. calls its newest railway, the £7 billion BAM—Baikal-Amur Mainline. The boast is justified. The BAM stretches 3,200 kilometres from a point west of Siberia's Lake Baikal to the Amur River on the Pacific coast, crossing seven mountain ranges and spanning more than 3,700 gorges, swamps, streams and rivers. For two thirds of the way, the heavy-duty tracks have been laid over permafrost, frozen ground that can thaw and heave. They also cross one of the most earthquake-prone regions in the world; as many as 2,000 tremors a year buckle the tracks and cause landslides.

BAM was a "hero project"—a huge, demanding task undertaken to impress the world and inspire the Soviet people. Thousands of young workers were enlisted from all over the country. Labouring year-round, they laid about half a kilometre of track a day. Where in the early 70s there was wilderness, a decade later there was not only railway, but more than 60 boom towns—and the dream of opening Siberia to development was closer to reality.

**Bulldozers prepare a site for a prefabricated bridge; behind them runs the broad swath cut through virgin birch and pine forest for the Baikal-Amur Mainline.**

**A travelling advertisement for the Baikal-Amur Mainline covers the side of one of the red-painted carriages of the Trans-Siberian Railway, with which the BAM will connect.**

**Siberian Yakuts—part of the labour force drawn from the local population—lay a prefabricated section of track with the aid of a crane.**

Members of a work gang lever a
section of track into place. Some BAM
wages were three times the national
norm. Women—here in kerchiefs—
received the same pay as the men.

Visiting musicians from Latvia put on
a concert by the railway lines for
BAM workers during a rest break.

Working in glare-lit mud, labourers
complete the 1.2-kilometre-long
Nagornyy tunnel after 18 months of
drilling through granite and ice.

Gloveless mechanics use petrol that
has been heated to thaw and wash
chilled parts of a drill.

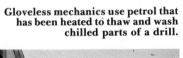

At temperatures of −45°C or lower, lorry engines must be left running day and night—or be warmed up by fires lighted underneath them.

Where insulating moss and lichens have been destroyed by construction work, the permafrost melts and becomes a bog. Long-term effects of such changes in the pristine ecology of Siberia are not yet known.

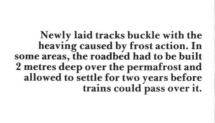

Newly laid tracks buckle with the heaving caused by frost action. In some areas, the roadbed had to be built 2 metres deep over the permafrost and allowed to settle for two years before trains could pass over it.

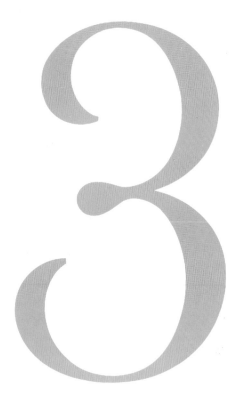

These faces from the Soviet Union present a small sample of its ethnic diversity: a Russian schoolgirl, a Georgian farm woman and an Uzbek worker from Central Asia. Ethnic identity is still felt strongly in many regions despite decades of intermarriage.

# A COUNTRY OF COUNTRIES

Most people the world over refer to the Soviet Union as Russia. Even Soviet citizens—who resent foreigners' use of the term—often call it by that name themselves. Its real name, the Union of Soviet Socialist Republics, mouthful though it is, reflects more nearly the country's human composition. It is not one country so much as many— a conglomeration of so-called union republics, autonomous republics and autonomous regions and areas.

In the U.S.S.R. as a whole, there are more than 100 ethnic groups, ranging from Russians and Mongolians to Uzbeks and Yakuts, speaking no fewer than 80 different languages, writing in five different alphabets, and practising Islam, Judaism, Buddhism and 152 sectarian versions of Christianity.

The extraordinary diversity of this multiracial land was most dramatically exposed in the late 1980s when President Gorbachev's new policy of *glasnost* released the long-festering resentments of different national and ethnic groups. Suddenly the world's last empire was under siege from within—facing territorial claims by Crimean Tartars, demands for independence from Georgians, Estonians, Moldavians, Latvians and Lithuanians, and various outbreaks of mass violence that ranged from civil war between Christian Armenians and Muslim Azerbaijanis to attacks by Uzbeks on minority Meshketian Turks.

All of these disparate peoples, and others, were forcefully demonstrating how, despite decades of Russification, they had retained an acute awareness of their own, distinctly separate, ethnic and cultural identity. In the case of Estonia, Latvia and Lithuania—the relatively prosperous Baltic states that Stalin seized in 1940—the desire of the people to have independence restored was so patently overwhelming that their secession from the Soviet Union came to be seen as an inevitability.

To the world at large, such widespread assertion of ethnic individuality seemed astonishing. But for Soviet citizens it came as much less of a surprise in the light of the Kremlin's less rigid controls. In the Soviet Union, ethnic background—which is generally translated as "nationality"— has always been as important as citizenship. Indeed, practically all official documents, including the interior passport that everyone is required to carry, specify both.

A Western visitor to Moscow got a hint of this ethnic preoccupation when he commented to his guide on the many Russian tourists in Red Square. She quickly corrected him. "Those are not Russians," she sneered, "those are Soviets." Her tone explained why the Soviet Union, despite its composite nature, is generally referred to as Russia. The Russians themselves may be only one

# 3

of a hundred ethnic groups, but they remain the most dominant people, their influence having spread to every part of the huge Soviet territory.

The Russians are descendants of Slavic tribes who settled in northern central Europe in prehistoric times and over the centuries mixed with various conquerors: Scandinavian, Lithuanian, Polish and German peoples from the west and, from the south and east, Tartars (also called Mongols), Khazars and others. The Russians remain predominantly Slavic, and intensely proud of that heritage. They are the most numerous of the Soviet peoples, 148 million strong, making up 51 per cent of the population of 289 million.

In addition, it is the Russians who inhabit the largest of the country's republics. Known officially as the Russian Soviet Federated Socialist Republic, or R.S.F.S.R., it spreads from the Baltic Sea to the shores of the Pacific Ocean, encompasses about three quarters of the Soviet Union's total landmass, and is the site of the largest industrial centres and cities, including the national capital, Moscow.

The Russians' influence beyond the R.S.F.S.R. is evident. Russian is taught in all the schools, and the Moscow accent is now the standard for radio and television. Nearly all the members of the Politburo, the ruling body of the Soviet Union, are Russians, and 91 per cent of the generals who were appointed between 1940 and 1976 were either Ukrainian or Russian.

The Russians came to such dominance by first conquering the Slavic groups neighbouring the Moscow region, and then going on to extend the borders of their country until, by 1881, it covered much the same terri-

tory as the U.S.S.R. does today. In the republics beyond the R.S.F.S.R., where non-Russians make up practically the entire population, control over local government was placed in the hands of the Russian representatives of the Communist Party. The top post, of first party secretary, would often be filled by a native inhabitant, but that person was generally a figurehead, the real power being wielded by a second party secretary—virtually always a

Russian—and by the local chief of the secret police, also a Russian. More often than not, neither of the Moscow representatives were able to speak the native language.

In the process, the Russians became masters of the multitude of peoples, Asians as well as Europeans, who continue to give the Soviet Union a rich diversity—and an inner pressure—unlike that of any other society in the world. Some of these peoples are quite

western city of Lvov, in a joyous commemoration of their brief existence as a sovereign state.

The Ukrainians consider themselves more cultivated than the Russians, and they take pleasure in reminding them that the Ukrainian city of Kiev was the country's capital when Moscow was "a wheel track in the forest". There are 42 million Ukrainians, and they make a big contribution to Soviet life.

Kiev, which the Russians call "the mother of cities", is today the third largest city in the U.S.S.R. Heavily damaged during World War II, it has now been restored as a handsome capital of culture, with poplar-lined avenues, theatres, an opera house, a symphony hall and a university, with 6,000 students who prefer to speak and write Ukrainian rather than Russian.

Much of the colour of the old Ukraine survives in the countryside, where comfortable white-washed mud-brick or stone houses with thatched roofs are decorated with the elaborate embroidery for which the region is famous. Here is found the rich, black top-soil that has made the Ukraine the breadbasket of the nation, and, now that sugar beets have become a major crop, the sugar bowl as well. Here also are the centres of the coalmining, steel and chemical industries.

The Ukrainians have long known how to make the most of their bounty. "My grandmother always said," boasts one housewife, "that a girl should be able to sift flour before she can walk and make bread before she can talk." A plate-sized loaf of bread called a *khlib i sil*, its centre cradling a small mound of salt, is still offered to guests as a symbol of hospitality.

When French novelist Honoré de Balzac visited the Ukraine, more than

different from the Russians; others are much like them in appearance, life-style and habits. But even those who seem to be most similar display distinctions in outlook.

Just south and west of the Russian homeland is that of their close relatives, the Ukrainians and the Belorussians, both Slavic groups that have long been part of the Russian Empire. The Belorussians, numbering approximately 8.5 million, have been assimi-

lated to some extent into the Russian culture, but the Ukrainians remain passionately proud of their own unique heritage and they resent any Russian condescension towards them.

The Ukrainians have never forgotten that between 1917 and 1919 they enjoyed short spells of national independence. In January 1990, during the heady days of *glasnost*, some 100,000 Ukrainians joined hands, forming a 475-kilometre chain from Kiev to the

# 3

a century ago, he observed, "I counted 77 ways of making bread." And when a Ukrainian heard of the Frenchman's comment, he added, "No one has counted all our cakes."

The Ukrainians, Belorussians and Russians form the Slavic nucleus of the country, making up 72 per cent of its population. Directly south of the Ukraine is another trio of peoples—Georgians, Armenians and Azerbaijanis—who occupy the Caucasus, the region that lies between the Black Sea and the Caspian and is traversed by the Caucasus Mountains. This territory became Russian by a series of annexations from 1801 to 1878. After World War I, Armenia, Azerbaijan and Georgia were recognized as independent states, but in 1921 they were incorporated into the U.S.S.R. The peoples who are the main occupants of these three countries are descended from Middle Easterners, with a touch of the Tartars who overran their mountainous homelands centuries ago. The most famous of their sons is Joseph Stalin, a Georgian.

Despite their proximity, the Georgians, Armenians and Azerbaijanis are very distinct ethnically and linguistically. And since 1989, the age-old conflicts between these peoples—especially those between Armenians and Azerbaijanis—have exploded into violence. Encouraged by *glasnost*, the Armenians mounted a number of mass demonstrations in protest at the Azerbaijanis' treatment of their people in the enclave of Nagorno Karabakh. The Azerbaijanis subsequently replied with an economic blockade, and the dispute continued to escalate into the greatest civil unrest since the establishment of Soviet power in Central Asia in the 1920s.

In peaceful times, the Transcaucasian peoples are an enterprising bunch. Their region produces wine, fruit, wheat, maize, barley, tea, hy-droelectric power, and, in the Baku fields of Azerbaijan, oil. All three peoples are noted for their free-wheeling activities, which frequently violate not only the spirit but also the letter of the Soviet law. For example, an Azerbaijani taxi driver candidly confesses that he once made a 500-rouble payoff to a housing minister to get his tiny, old-fashioned house. A modern flat in one of the new high-rise buildings outside the city would have required a bribe beyond his means, he explains. Why did he not simply apply to get on the official waiting list? He laughingly replies that the wait would have been 20 to 30 years.

Over the years, *Pravda* has regularly printed disapproving stories about such illicit dealings. A construction co-operative was accused of having bulldozed an unauthorized road over the Caucasus into the R.S.F.S.R. just so farmers could dodge the "vegetable patrols" set up on the main road by the authorities to put a stop to illegal transacting of food. Large amounts of money were at stake; at least one farmer was known to have made an illegal profit of 50,000 roubles, selling 10 tonnes of tangerines.

In 1973, a national scandal arose when a Georgian, Otari Lazeishvili, was accused of having pocketed a million roubles—money that should rightfully have gone to the state—by running an underground factory network manufacturing such goods as turtle-neck jumpers and trendy rain-coats for his 100 collaborators to sell in black markets across the Soviet Union.

Georgians are noted for their wine-making, and they take deep pleasure in food and drink. When a diner selects wine in a Georgian restaurant, the waiter is likely to ask "How many

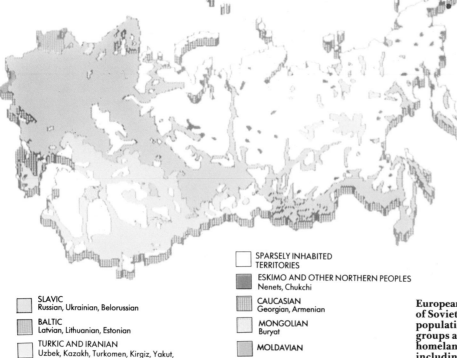

SPARSELY INHABITED
TERRITORIES

ESKIMO AND OTHER NORTHERN PEOPLES
Nenets, Chukchi

CAUCASIAN
Georgian, Armenian

MONGOLIAN
Buryat

MOLDAVIAN

SLAVIC
Russian, Ukrainian, Belorussian

BALTIC
Latvian, Lithuanian, Estonian

TURKIC AND IRANIAN
Uzbek, Kazakh, Turkomen, Kirgiz, Yakut,
Tartar, Azerbaijani, Tadzhik

**European Slavs are the most numerous of Soviet peoples (72 per cent of the population). Although most ethnic groups are concentrated in their homelands, many different peoples—including millions of Russians—are dispersed all over the country.**

bottles?'' This love of conviviality is traced, in one charming account, to the origin of the Georgian homeland. On the eighth day of Creation, goes this story, God parcelled out the globe to the many peoples of the world. Then he started for home, whereupon he encountered the Georgians, sitting round a table by the roadside.

Shaking his head, God admonished them. ''While you sat here eating and drinking, singing and joking, the whole world was divided up. Now nothing is left for you.'' Their leader, with true Georgian cunning, replied, ''It was very wrong, we know. But God, while we enjoyed ourselves, we didn't forget you. We drank to you to thank you for such a beautiful world.''

''That's more than anybody else did,'' said God. ''So I'll tell you what I'm going to do. I'm going to give you the last little corner of the world—the place I was saving for myself because it is most like Paradise.''

The Armenians have an equally colourful tale of the Creation. According to the Armenian account, by the time God reached them while making his distribution of the earth's land, he had nothing left but rocks—and rocks are what they got. Theirs is a rugged, stark country with most of the arable land squeezed into the Aras Valley along the border with Turkey.

The Armenians, Azerbaijanis and Georgians claim to get a special bonus from living where they do—incredible longevity. The Soviet government calls the Caucasus a centre of the *dolgozhiteli* (long-lifers), people who remain hale after more than 100 years. According to the Kiev Institute of Gerontology, there are some 20,000 long-lifers in the U.S.S.R., a major portion of them living in Georgia and Azerbaijan.

**Farm women harvest cabbage on an Armenian hillside below an old stone church. The Armenian Apostolic Church, one of the most venerable of Christian denominations, has its own hierarchy and rituals, distinct from those of Russian Orthodoxy.**

# 3

An Azerbaijani gerontologist, called Shukur Gasanov, attributes the supposed longevity of his countrymen to their simple ways: "They are early risers and they work all the time. Their diet relies mostly on vegetables and milk products—sour milk, kefir, curds and our soft white cheese. They eat many greens and especially fruits such as grapes and apricots. And they also fast to rest their stomachs. They drink natural spring water. They stay on the move, and spend much time in the open air. Even when it is cold, they bathe often in our cold rivers. They always sleep on hard beds. And not too long—perhaps six hours a night."

The widely touted virtues of these habits in prolonging life have been repeatedly investigated by Westerners (and a few sceptical Russians). One authority who checked back is Dr. Alexander Leaf, Professor of Clinical Medicine at the Massachusetts General Hospital in Boston. On a visit to the Caucasus in 1975, he was impressed by the health and advanced years of the elderly he saw, and he returned to write a book, *Youth in Old Age*, that generally confirmed the claims of great longevity.

Continuing to follow the cases that he had observed, however, Dr. Leaf became suspicious. One woman who claimed to be 109 years old also told him that she had given birth when she was 55. Dr. Leaf then discovered that her baby boy was a stepson. Studying issues of *Pravda*, which regularly publishes photographs of *dolgozhiteli* celebrating their 140th, 150th or 160th birthday, he noticed that an obituary of one long-lifer, Shirali Mislimov, was followed in succeeding years by the same picture of Mislimov, congratulating him each time on his birthday.

A Georgian "long-lifer" flaunts his fitness by performing a traditional dance. Claims that natives of the Caucasus Mountains enjoy remarkable longevity are often made—and just as often disputed.

"The last time, he was 170," said a disillusioned Dr. Leaf. He finally came to the conclusion that the claims of remarkable longevity were, at best, exaggerated. "I was gullible," he said.

More exotic to Westerners are the ways of the peoples living to the east, in the arid lands of Central Asia, which make up nearly 18 per cent of the total area of the U.S.S.R. Here the impact of the Orient is visible to the outsider in the desert robes of the men, the women who still wear their black, shiny hair in long plaits, the felt-covered yurts, or round tents, of the countryside and the ubiquitous tea-houses and mosques of the cities.

And yet, even in this faraway eastern land, the signs of transition to the modern world of western Russia are everywhere evident in the clusters of high-rise buildings and the sprawling complexes of smoke-spewing factories.

This vast stretch of desert, grasslands and mountains—which reaches from the Caspian Sea all the way to the border of China—is redolent with the exotic history of trade routes and camel trains, of army outposts and cavalry, of Marco Polo and Genghis Khan. This was the major link between China and the West, as well as the route of invasion taken by Cyrus and Alexander. And it was a land of poets and potentates long before most Slavs were able to read and write. By the 16th century, however, there was a change: galleons sailing the Indian Ocean had replaced the caravans; therefore the region soon lost its profitable trade and slipped into desperate poverty, its people struggling to survive.

Today, with the help of Soviet technology—and Russian technicians—Central Asia has been transformed into a productive and populous area.

**Uzbek girls show off glossy black hair, coiffed into 40 plaits under gold-embroidered caps called *doppi*.**

So many Russian settlers have been sent to Kazakhstan to farm in the Virgin Lands Programme, for example, that the population, 6.5 million in 1950, doubled by 1980; in Alma-Ata, the capital of Kazakhstan, two thirds of the residents are ethnic Russians.

Nevertheless, the influx of Russians has not overwhelmed the descendants of the Tartars. In fact, the opposite may be true. With improved sanitation and health facilities, the Asian birth rate has gone up and is now double that of the Russians. By the year 2000 it may be six times as great. By then, it is estimated, the Russians' 51 per cent majority in the U.S.S.R. as a whole will have slipped to about a 46 per cent share, and the Central Asians, now accounting for 16 per cent of the total, will make up 21 per cent.

Along the northern reaches of Central Asia, Kazakhstan is home to 200,000 nomadic shepherds, who pack their yurts on to their horses and travel with the seasons, like their ancestors for centuries before them. But many others now are settled farmers, tending newly developed fields that produce a fifth of all the grain that is harvested in the Soviet Union.

To the south-west, Turkmenistan—90 per cent of which lies in the Kara-Kum desert—has been altered in another way. Now the Kara-Kum has been made to bloom with cotton, vegetables and alfalfa (for vast herds of karakul sheep) by a giant canal that cuts through the desert, bringing water from the Amu Darya River and the Aral Sea all the way to Ashkhabad and Turkmenistan's western border.

The canal, which is 800 kilometres long, 90 metres wide and 4.5 metres deep, took eight years to complete. "Our old people had never believed that water could cross the Kara-Kum," said one Turkoman. "When it flowed in, they had to touch it—to dip their hands in it. Some of them began to pray. We feasted for two months."

The snow-capped Pamir mountains rise to the east of Turkmenistan, and in the valleys and on the slopes live the Tadzhiks. Visitors remark on the handsome men and beautiful women, with their long black eyelashes and lithe figures. They too have been brought rapidly into line with the industrial age; Tadzhik cotton fields have the highest yield in the Soviet Union, and Tadzhikistan has a thoroughly modern textile industry. But many Tadzhiks still prefer the nomadic existence of the goatherd, pursuing with their animals the seasonal supplies of grass and water. Their ancestors' yurts, however, have largely been replaced by modern lightweight tents, equipped with transistor radios blaring Middle Eastern music.

To the north and east is Kirgizia, the U.S.S.R.'s Wild West, a republic of horses and horse-lovers, with a population of about two million of the latter and 265,000 of the former. Horses gallop their way through Kirgiz folklore, and they are still used here for tending sheep in the rocky pasturelands of the mountains, and cattle in the valleys. Horses are also raised for meat—though, says a Kirgiz cowboy, "A Kirgiz would not eat a horse if it had ever been saddled—never!" Horse breeding and cattle raising continue to be important activities, although today they have been collectivized.

Modern industry has been introduced to Kirgizia. The region now has sugar-beet farms, textile mills and machinery factories in the valleys, and they are connected to coal mines in the mountains by paved roads.

The most striking examples of the

# 3

coalescing of old and new can be seen in the heartland of Central Asian culture, Uzbekistan. The home of the Uzbeks lies exactly athwart the old Silk Road, which once carried trade from the Black Sea in Europe across Central Asia to north-western China. Evidence of Uzbek glory can still be seen, including the mosaic-covered minarets of the great Tamerlane's mausoleum in the ancient capital of Samarkand. Partly restored, it is now surrounded by tall office buildings and flats.

A little more than 200 kilometres from Samarkand is the modern Uzbek capital of Tashkent, the largest industrial city in Central Asia. Much of Tashkent was destroyed in 1966 when a series of earthquakes, whose epicentre was directly beneath the city, struck without warning. A modern metropolis has replaced the ancient buildings reduced to rubble. Despite the threat of more quakes, there is an underground railway system.

In these 20th-century surroundings, the Uzbeks continue many of their old ways. In restaurants, the background accompaniment often is not music but an elder sitting on a platform reading aloud excerpts from poetry or newspapers, as was the custom in the days when literacy was rare. In open markets, independent suppliers, competing with the prices of the state stores, haggle with their customers over plate-shaped loaves of bread, red peppers, plums, apples and melons.

When an Uzbek woman comes back home from her factory job in the evening, she is likely to change from her contemporary clothes to her *atlas* (a

Living in a modern house but sitting, like their nomad ancestors, on a Bukhara rug, an Uzbek family shares a meal. The dish is *palov*—finger food of rice, mutton and vegetables moulded into bite-sized balls.

74

long, loose blouse) and a pair of pantaloons; though she and her husband may be able to afford a modern stove, she may well prefer to cook her *manty, plov* and *lepeski* (dumplings, pilaff and bread) in a stone oven set on the earthen floor of her open kitchen.

Uzbeks and Kazakhs, Armenians and Azerbaijanis, Ukrainians and Belorussians, are major ethnic peoples largely concentrated in major geographical areas. Scattered across the U.S.S.R. are dozens of smaller groups: Tuvans and Buryats, Udegays, Kets and Komi, Orocks, Aleuts and Ainu. None is more individualistic than the hardy Northern peoples of Siberia, known as the Chukchis and Yakuts.

Most of the aborigines of north-west Siberia were still virtually in the Stone Age at the beginning of the 20th century. Tsarist Russia had done little

or nothing to introduce them to modern ways. The Soviet government began with a programme of formal education, providing an alphabet—Latin at first but changed to Cyrillic in 1937. Itinerant teachers attempted to follow the nomadic groups, but this proved to be impractical and the government established boarding schools.

As more and more children became educated, some went on to Soviet universities. One of these students was Yuri Rytkheu, a Chukchi who is a popular Soviet novelist. His recollections of childhood days on Cape Dezhnev, situated across the Bering Strait from Alaska, evoke the primitive ways of these people of the Soviet Arctic.

"Our whole life was bound up with the sea," Rytkheu writes. "Early in the morning the hunters set off to sea. In winter they hid themselves in the light

blue twilight, among the masses of broken ice, to hunt seals. In summer the hunters set off into the sparkling patches of sunlight and among the floating icebergs to chase the herds of whales and walruses."

The Chukchis, Rytkheu reports, lived in *yarangi*, portable circular tents that resemble yurts but which are covered with walrus hide. Walrus tusks at one time provided the runners for their sleighs and "tips of harpoons, handles of knives and numerous other instruments were also fashioned from this strong ivory. Walrus and whale oil burned in stone lamps, warming and illuminating our home. Our entire view of the world, our philosophy, fairy tales, legends and songs were linked with the sea and its animals."

Rytkheu remembers how the 20th century intruded on this ancient way

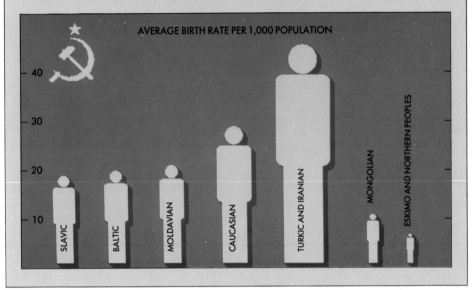

## A GROWING ASIAN POPULATION

The birth rate among ethnic Russians has been declining, while that of the Soviet Union's Turkic and Iranian peoples of Central Asia has been rising. This increase in births in the eastern U.S.S.R. is due partly to a reduction in infant mortality in the region but mainly to the tradition of large families among the Muslims.

The Russian birth rate is below the national average of 19.9 per thousand; if the trend continues, the Russians will be a minority in the Soviet Union by the year 2000.

**AVERAGE BIRTH RATE PER 1,000 POPULATION**

40 — 30 — 20 — 10 —

SLAVIC — BALTIC — MOLDAVIAN — CAUCASIAN — TURKIC AND IRANIAN — MONGOLIAN — ESKIMO AND NORTHERN PEOPLES

of life, recalling that the Chukchi saw aeroplanes before they saw horse-drawn carriages and trains. Soviet ministers came to study the Chukchis as well as to educate them, and members of Rytkheu's tribe joked about the "typical family here: father, mother, two children, as well as, over there in the corner of the hut, the researcher."

Today's Chukchis have moved into the modern world, some of them even flying from one fishing spot to another by helicopter. They may still live in a *yaranga* but it is now likely to contain recent newspapers and magazines, and at its entrance waits a radio-equipped snowmobile. The children go off to boarding school in the autumn and return in the spring.

Some of the Chukchis are reindeer herders. They—and the Evenks, Yakuts and Nenets around the Arctic Circle west of European Lapland—continue to pursue this seasonal

nomadic occupation, folding away their *yarangi* and following the herds through the summer nights while the reindeer fatten up for the winter.

Reindeer, as Rytkheu points out, are marvellously well adapted to life in this part of the world. They "graze the most meagre pastures, and despite all this, they manage by the end of the summer to build up enough of a layer of fat to survive the harsh winter."

But in their own nomadic feeding patterns, arctic reindeer range over wide areas. So when the Soviets tried in the 1930s to collectivize reindeer herding, they found it far more difficult than they had anticipated. For two decades, the government strove to herd the herders into villages. But while the humans could be forced, the reindeer could not; the animals persisted in following their non-collective feeding routes. Faced with being left behind without the animals, many

herders killed their reindeer.

Finally, the Soviet authorities saw that they would have to compromise: they collectivized the production and distribution of reindeer meat but allowed the herders to follow their wandering animals. The reindeer herds of the Soviet Arctic, which had declined from two million in 1929 to about half that number in the early 1950s, had by the early 1980s recovered to approximately 1.5 million.

But few ethnic groups were able to come to terms with the Soviet government as successfully as the reindeer herders. During World War II, several mass deportations took place. The 1.5 million Volga Germans—descendants of settlers who had come to Russia during the 18th century—were uprooted from their homes in the Volga region and resettled in Central Asia and Siberia. The government feared that they would collaborate with the German invaders. Although there was no evidence of treason, they were also deprived of citizenship, which was not restored until 1955.

One group of Muslim Tartars, the descendants of Bhatu Khan's Golden Horde who ruled Russia for two centuries, suffered a similar fate. Next to the Uzbeks, the Tartars are the largest non-Slavic group in the Soviet Union, and nearly every major city in the U.S.S.R. had a Tartar community. However, during World War II, the Tartars in the Crimea were accused of collaborating with the Nazi occupation forces. In the course of just a few hours on May 18, 1944, every man, woman and child—some 200,000 in all—was picked up and then deported from the Crimea; the great majority were sent to Uzbekistan. Their homes were levelled, and all evidence of their

**Workers on a collective farm close to the Mongolian border step outside their front door to greet a visitor. The dry steppe is grazing land—mainly for cattle and sheep.**

# 3

existence, including street signs, was obliterated. Like the Volga Germans, they were stripped of their citizenship.

In the 1960s, in an amazingly bold act, 120,000 Crimean Tartars signed a petition asking for their homeland to be returned to them, while 15,000 sent letters and telegrams to government officials. When nothing happened, they organized a second petition of 115,000 names and dispatched 20,000 letters and telegrams. A delegation sent to Moscow was arrested, sparking off rioting in Uzbekistan. Finally, 4,000 Tartars journeyed to Moscow at the peak of the tourist season and staged a demonstration: it caught the attention of the foreigners present—and the Kremlin. A month later they were given back their citizenship, but not their Crimean homeland.

Two decades later, in 1987, the Tartars were the first group to take advantage of *glasnost* to publicize their grievances. In Moscow, they staged a week-long demonstration until the Kremlin agreed to set up a commission to investigate their demand to return to their homeland. The commission duly recognized that they had been victims of an injustice. It did nothing to make amends, but at least they had been given a sympathetic hearing, and now the floodgates were wide open to a torrent of demands from other nationalistic populations throughout the land.

At the same time, relaxation of restrictions allowed a resurgence of ethnic religions. Christians, Muslims, Buddhists and Jews now experienced greater freedom of expression than at any time since the 1920s. The price of this freedom was accentuation of ethnic differences and a rekindling of age-old animosities.

*Glasnost* also helped the Orthodox Church to prosper in the Russian homeland *(page 108)* and to reassert its traditional influence as priests and church members became candidates in local council elections. But in 1989, by visiting the Pope in the Vatican, President Gorbachev inflamed the long-simmering rivalry between the Russian Orthodox and the Ukrainian Greek-Catholic Church. That year also saw bitter fighting between Christian Armenians and Muslim Azerbaijanis; and increasing anti-Semitism as Soviet citizens sought scapegoats for the failure of economic reforms.

The revival of Islamic expression was especially significant because the Muslims of the Soviet Union—an estimated 55 million—constitute the world's fifth largest Islamic population (after Indonesia, Pakistan, Bangladesh and India). In the past, the Soviets had generally been wary of the Muslim religion, knowing that it could generate explosively anti-Russian feelings.

In 1917, only weeks after the Communists took over, Lenin soothingly announced to the nation's Muslims, "Your religion and customs, your national and cultural institutions are proclaimed free and inviolable." But the Communists' suspicion of religion quickly made a mockery of Lenin's promises. Eventually, most of the country's 26,000 mosques and 24,000 religious schools were shut down. The vast majority of Islamic teachers were either killed or imprisoned. During World War II, Stalin forcibly deported to Siberia entire populations of Muslims who were suspected of disloyalty.

Yet, with only 300 mosques to serve the tens of millions in Central Asia, travelling mullahs continued to perform the religious rites, and the number of secret Muslim societies grew rather than declined. Moreover, the birth rate among Muslims was always increasing while that of ethnic Russians steadily declined. In the late 1980s, the government's greater tolerance of Islam was tacit recognition of the importance attached to Muslim co-operation in bringing about an economic revival.

Many new mosques were now opened, and there was official discouragement of anti-Muslim propaganda. But, curiously, there remained

From a minaret in Bukhara, in the region of Uzbekistan, a muezzin issues a call to prayer. His congregation are among the 55 million Muslims of the Soviet Union, most of whom live in Central Asia.

a lack of Muslim solidarity in the Soviet Union. In 1989, for example, hostility surfaced between a variety of Muslim groups: Tajiks clashed with Kirgiz over land and water rights; Kazakhs in Novyy Uzen attacked shop-owners from the Caucasus; Uzbeks rampaged against Meskhetian Turks; Muslim Kurds sided with Armenians against the Muslim Azerbaijanis. The scores of Muslim peoples scattered across the mountainous Trans-caucasus and plains of Central Asia clearly felt that they had little in common except their religion and their Soviet citizenship.

Meanwhile, for the Soviet Union's two million Jews, the reforms of the late 1980s were very much a mixed blessing. Judaism has for centuries been the most persecuted of religions in Russia. Ironically, after generations of pogroms, consignment to ghettos, and other more subtle forms of dis-crimination, the early days of the Soviet state had brought an improve-ment in the fortunes of Russian Jews; they had prospered as fully fledged citizens at last. The Jewish State Theatre was founded in 1919 (the painter Marc Chagall was its stage designer); nearly 20 other Yiddish-language theatre groups sprouted up around the Soviet Union. Yiddish newspapers were published in Moscow and at least three other Soviet cities.

However, anti-Semitism returned under Stalin's rule; the country's 1,000 Jewish schools were closed and Jews found themselves discriminated against in their jobs. They responded by attempting to leave the U.S.S.R., but they were refused exit permits until the 1970s, when some 250,000 Jews were finally allowed to emigrate. By the 1990s, despite the presence of a

more tolerant, even protective, gov-ernment, the great exodus had risen to more than 100,000 in a single year.

For Jews, *glasnost* meant that their religious freedom was recognized by the state, and they were at last permitted to emigrate at will. But at the same time the dark forces of anti-Semitism were re-emerging—most notably in the form of Pamyat, an ex-treme nationalist group devoted to the restoration of pure Russian traditions. When it came into being in the early 1970s, Pamyat had been an under-ground movement embracing various factions, only one of which had fascist tendencies. But under *glasnost*, the right-wing ultranationalist voice within Pamyat won out. By allowing unortho-dox views to be expressed openly, *glas-nost* helped not only the Jews but also anti-Jewish organizations.

In repressing or tolerating religions, as in every relationship with this vast array of different ethnic groups, the overriding concern of the dominant Russians is political—the need to con-trol such a vibrant conglomeration of peoples. Each group is ambitious, proud of its past glories, certain of its

own superiority and resentful of the Russians' often arrogant oversight.

Tensions between the Russians and their not-quite-equal compatriots are always present and they frequently come to the surface. An American graduate student who had spent a year among the Uzbeks working on her doc-toral thesis recounts one such occur-rence in a department store. She asked, in Russian, for washing powder and put down a rouble to pay for it. "I only take exact change," announced the shop assistant. When the American re-plied that she did not have any change, the assistant shot back: "Then you'll just have to wear dirty underwear."

The woman was amazed. "I looked at him incredulously," she recalled, until finally he responded. "'Where are you from?' he asked, and when I told him America, he apologized pro-fusely. 'I thought you were Russian,' he said—and then gave me the wash-ing powder and my change. If I had been from Europe, China or even another Soviet republic, I could have bought that detergent. But for Rus-sians in Central Asia, it's very often 'exact change or dirty underwear.'"

An Armenian boy cradles a cockerel that will be blessed and sacrificed in thanks for prayers answered.

# PEOPLES AT WORK

By law, every citizen of the Soviet Union is entitled to a job. In a country that is so huge and is home to so many diverse ethnic groups, work can take an amazing variety of colourful and distinctive forms, from ballet dancing in Leningrad to herding goats in Central Asia.

Many of these tasks are carried out by native peoples in traditional ways; fruit sellers in the open market in the Muslim city of Tashkent look and work as they have for centuries. But many of their neighbours wear Western-style clothes in textile mills and machine factories, working alongside people who have only recently moved from other regions. Europeans, in particular, have gone east by the thousand to such lightly populated areas as Kazakhstan, to turn steppe into farmland, and to Yakutia, to exploit untapped mineral wealth. The extent of the shuffling of the Soviet peoples can be seen in marriage statistics: 30 per cent of all weddings unite brides and grooms of different ethnic ancestry.

**A Moscow model shows off a silver-fox coat. Fashion may not be a Soviet speciality, but furs are. The U.S.S.R. is the world's principal supplier of pelts, most of them from Siberia.**

Construction workers take a break at a Moscow building site. Eighty-five per cent of Soviet women hold jobs of some kind.

A Nenets reindeer herder ropes one of the 17,000 animals on his collective, near Arkhangelsk. The farm sells 350 tonnes of reindeer meat a year.

Full of youthful grace, a veteran ballet instructor in a Leningrad school conducts a class.

**Smoking a *papirosa*—a cigarette in a cardboard holder—a Ukrainian cowboy keeps his eye on the cattle he tends.**

A retired Ukrainian adds to his pension income by turning out combs in his home workshop. Such cottage industries supply many consumer goods.

A Georgian teacher listens to her student practising the official, standardized lesson.

A kosher butcher prepares meat in Georgia, home to a dwindling number of Soviet Jews.

Shirtless in the steamy atmosphere of a Georgian health spa, a masseur lathers a client for a rubdown.

In Siberia, a European runs a forklift.

A Tashkent street vendor sells pomegranates.

An animal breeder in the Kosh-Agach region of Siberia holds up a young goat, of a type raised for its warm, thick fleece.

Men of the Khevsur tribe, a fierce Georgian people who claimed descent from Crusaders, wear medieval chain mail in this 1890s photograph. They had been absorbed into the expanding Russian Empire at the beginning of the 19th century.

# A LONG AND VIOLENT HISTORY

*She was christened in childhood with a lash,
torn to pieces,
scorched.
Her soul was trampled by the feet,
inflicting blow upon blow,
of Pechenegs,
Varangians,
Tartars,
and our own people—
much more terrible than the Tartars.*

In these few lines from a poem published in 1963, Yevgeny Yevtushenko conveyed the history of Russia and, by extension, the history of the Soviet Union. A land unprotected by natural barriers, it has suffered invasion after invasion—from the east by Pechenegs, Tartars, Khazars and countless others, from the north and west by Varangians, Swedes, Lithuanians, Poles, French and Germans. It has been oppressed by its own rulers, who have included some of the cruellest tyrants the world has known. Such a history explains why the Russian people seem so passionately possessive of their land, so distrustful of foreigners, so submissive to authoritarian rule. "Russia's endurance became famous," wrote Yevtushenko. "She did endure."

The story begins in about 1,000 B.C. with the Cimmerians, farmers of the plains north of the Black Sea. Around 700 B.C., they were overrun by the first Asiatic horsemen, the Scythians, another long-vanished people, who left behind in burial mounds a fortune in golden ornaments—diadems, necklaces, bracelets, rings, earrings—that today are national treasures.

The Scythians in turn yielded to a new group of Asiatic nomads, the Sarmatians, and these were followed by the Goths and then the Huns; under their leader, Attila, the Huns went on to terrorize much of Europe, rampaging as far to the west as Orléans, where they were at last defeated by Visigoths and Gallo–Romans in 451 A.D. In the wake of the Huns came the Avars and then the Khazars.

The Khazars were traders, and among the peoples they dealt with were the Slavs, a group of slash-and-burn farmers and fur trappers living in the forested area of present-day Kiev, Novgorod and Moscow. Little is known of their earlier history. Related to other Slavic peoples of Central Europe, these Eastern Slavs waited out the Scythians, Sarmatians, Huns, Avars and other conquerors to become the enduring Russians, a name they acquired in a roundabout fashion during the ninth and 10th centuries.

The name was a Norse gift. Scandinavian traders, the Varangians, using the inland waterways of the Volkov and Dnieper Rivers to reach the rich market of Byzantium, passed right through the Slavic·heartland. In time, these Norsemen, one group of whom are believed to have been called the Rus, established trading posts in the Slavs' territory. Two of the trading posts,

# 4

Kiev and Novgorod, grew into fortified towns ruled by Norse princes. And Kiev, strategically located just where the Dnieper breaks out of the forests into the steppe, eventually became the thriving centre of the infant Kiev state, the ancestral home of modern Russia.

Around 980, Kiev was under the rule of Vladimir, the first of the long series of autocrats who shaped Russia to their will. By this time most of the rulers of Europe, the Near East and North Africa had adopted one or another of the great monotheistic religions. Europe and Byzantium were governed by Christians, the Arab world by Muslims; to the south of Kiev was the then independent state of the Khazars, whose rulers had adopted Judaism as their official religion. Vladimir felt that a single state faith could foster political unity, and he decided to impose one, replacing the numerous pagan beliefs practised in Russia. According to legend, he decreed the official faith only after sending emissaries to collect information on Islam, Judaism and Christianity.

The first he rejected because it prohibited wine. "Drinking," he said, "is the joy of the Russes." The second he spurned because the originators of Judaism had had to flee their homeland, and Vladimir saw no point in adopting the religion of a dispersed people.

That left just the two branches of Christianity. Vladimir's agents, investigating the Roman Catholic Church, "beheld no glory" in it. But in Byzantium they were dazzled by the Eastern Orthodox Church. "The Greeks led us to the buildings where they worshipped their God, and we knew not whether we were in heaven or on earth. For on earth there is no such splendour or such beauty, and we are at a loss to describe it." Impressed by this report, Vladimir arranged to be baptized into the Orthodox Church and forced all of his subjects to do the same.

Vladimir's choice of Eastern Orthodoxy over Western Catholicism had results of lasting significance. It isolated the country from the rest of Europe, provoked abiding suspicion of Western ideas, and incited tragic enmity between Russia and its Roman Catholic neighbours—particularly the Poles.

Vladimir's bold stroke did indeed give the Kiev state a measure of unity. But not for long. Constantly battered by waves of nomadic invaders, it succumbed to the Tartars, who in the 13th century conquered much of Europe and Asia. The Tartars ruled Russia for more than 200 years, and the fledgling Russian state was reduced to a few small principalities paying tribute to their Tartar masters but tenuously linked by the Orthodox Church.

Kiev, in the midst of the Tartar-held Ukrainian region, was never to regain its political supremacy, although it remains today a principal centre of Soviet culture and commerce. Many modern Ukrainians, while claiming credit for the founding of Russia, do not consider themselves Russians. They are, they insist, Ukrainians, and they are a bit scornful of the neighbouring Slavs to the north, the Russians who took advantage of the Tartar conquest to gain the power they hold today.

These northern Slavs peopled the principality then known as Muscovy, its chief town a nondescript wooden settlement called Moscow. The Muscovites were only loosely controlled by the Tartars but acknowledged their dominance and paid them tribute. Muscovite princes, cannily using their tribute-paying role to better their own position, collected taxes for their overlords but pocketed some of the take. Eventually they were strong enough to challenge the Tartars.

By a fluke, they were also able to supplant Kiev as the spiritual capital of Russia. The head of the Russian Church, on tour, happened to die in Moscow, and the Muscovite princes seized the opportunity to persuade his successor to transfer his seat from Kiev to Moscow. Thus fortified with temporal and spiritual power, Muscovy finally threw off Tartar rule in 1380, and by 1462 a potent Moscow prince, Ivan III, asserted his authority over Novgorod and Kiev as well as Moscow, so uniting the Slavic principalities into the Russian nation. Ivan took to calling himself Tsar—the Russian equivalent to Caesar, which was the title of the Emperors of Rome. His contemporaries referred to him as Ivan the Great.

Although Ivan III was an autocrat, he ruled with an even hand. The same cannot be said about his grandson,

Ivan IV, whose rule was so tyrannical that he is remembered as Ivan the Terrible. The Russian word *"grozny"*, which is translated as "terrible", actually means "awesome", and indeed there was a kind of grandeur in Ivan's excesses. Towards the end of his 51-year reign, which was the longest in Russian history, he was probably mad.

There was much in Ivan's childhood to account for such an end. At three, he lost his father; when he was seven, his mother died under mysterious circumstances, supposedly poisoned. Members of two boyar, or noble, families, the Bielskys and Shuiskys, seized power as his regents. In public they accorded him respect, but in private they treated him, in his own words, "as a menial", denying him food and clothes while they ransacked the imperial treasury. Murders, executions and unexplained imprisonments were commonplace. One night the boy Ivan was awakened by soldiers who burst into his bedroom looking for a priest they had been ordered to kill.

Ivan took part in formal state affairs from the age of five, and when he was 13 years old, he donned the official robes of the Tsar and presided over meetings of the Bielsky and Shuisky regents. In that role, he proved anything but pliable. At one meeting he delivered a routine criticism of mismanagement and waste; then, taking advantage of bickering among the regents, he did something utterly unexpected: he singled out one regent, Andrei Shuisky, and ordered him to be arrested. When the astonished Shuisky tried to escape, he was clubbed to death by palace dogkeepers, whom the young Ivan had befriended. Ivan had not intended Shuisky's death, only his capture, but the boy took responsibility for the

murder and indeed capitalized on it, gathering more and more autocratic power to himself.

When he was 16, Ivan was crowned Tsar in a ceremony that he ensured had the maximum pomp. Three times he was showered with gold and silver coins, to symbolize the prosperity that would distinguish his reign. Bells pealed throughout the country. Three weeks later he was married to Anastasia Zakharina-Romanov, a member of a titled family that was subsequently to play a central role in Russian history. Anastasia was beautiful and intelligent, and Ivan adored her.

Many historians divide Ivan's reign into a good half and a bad half. Ivan took all real power away from the boyars and governed singlehandedly and dictatorially. However, in the first years of his rule, the benign and progressive half, he called a general assembly made up of boyars from many noble families and issued edicts based on their advice. He required this hereditary aristocracy to supply soldiers to the army, easing a burden that had been borne entirely by the landed gentry. A learned man himself, he ordered rare manuscripts to be imported,

established presses to publish books, and set scholars to work translating Russian manuscripts into other languages to show the world that Russia was not backward. And he recommended that music—one of his abiding passions—be taught in all schools.

Ivan simultaneously pressed against the Tartars still controlling Russian lands and sent his troops to conquer other peoples, beginning the expansion of the Empire. In 1555, to celebrate the final rout of the Tartars in Kazan, he caused a great church to be built in Moscow's Red Square, the extravagantly ornate St. Basil's. Actually a cluster of nine chapels forming an eight-point star, it is topped by fancifully carved steeples and cupolas of varying heights and colours, based on the wooden architecture of traditional churches, though in fact made of stone.

Ivan's grandiose gestures extended even to the table. He thought nothing of presiding over five- and six-hour banquets for hundreds—sometimes thousands—of guests, each of whom he greeted on arrival by name. Dinner on such occasions was served on gem-encrusted gold and silver plates, and guests drank from cornelian goblets or from reindeer horns and ostrich eggshells. The food was similarly lavish. Roast swan might be followed by roast peacock, goose with millet, spiced crane and sturgeon. Between courses the servants changed livery, and Ivan himself often changed crowns.

In 1560, Anastasia died mysteriously, and the bad half of Ivan's reign began. He was convinced the Tsarina had been murdered. His mind seemed to shatter, and he sank into a life of dissipation and paranoia. Anyone whom he even remotely suspected of plotting against him was executed and in 1571

A roast swan in full plumage is brought to lavishly dressed guests toasting a bashful bride in this 19th-century painting. Such extravagant and often lengthy feasts were a tradition of the Russian aristocracy; one that was given by Ivan the Terrible went on for three days.

he ordered thousands of citizens of Novgorod to be killed when civil unrest disturbed that city.

In order to protect himself against "traitors", Ivan established a personal security force, the *oprichniki*—the first of Russia's infamous secret police forces. Dressed in black and riding coal-black horses, this band of men, eventually 6,000 strong, rode the countryside to find and destroy anyone suspected of disloyalty to Ivan. Whole towns were wiped out and even a cousin of the Tsar was murdered, together with his family. Then, in another fateful move late in his reign, Ivan began exiling his political opponents to newly conquered Siberia.

Banishment to Siberia may have been better than the punishment dealt out in Moscow, where Ivan's supposed enemies were likely to be tortured sadistically. Ivan personally took part. When he was particularly angry, said an observer, he foamed at the mouth like a horse. During one such violent episode, he struck his eldest son on the head with a staff. The Tsarevich died a few days later, leaving Ivan demented with grief. He became obsessed with knowing when he himself would die, and in 1584 he sent for 60 witches from Lapland, who obliged him by specifying a date. His death would come, they said, on March 18 of that same year. On March 18, Ivan duly suffered a seizure and within minutes was "stark dead", as Sir Jerome Horsey, the English Ambassador to Ivan's court, put it.

Ivan's death began a generation of chaos, called the Time of Troubles, marked by dynastic struggles, social upheaval and foreign intrusion. Ivan's weak, incompetent son Fyodor came to the throne, but power was held by Fyodor's brother-in-law, Boris Godunov (subject of the opera of that name), who is said to have reinforced his position by killing Fyodor's heir Dmitri. Boris was eventually crowned Tsar, but then came one of the most bizarre episodes in history: two pretenders claimed in succession to be the murdered Dmitri, still alive.

The two false Dmitris were both sponsored by Poland, which had long contested the ownership of Russia's western lands, and which during the Time of Troubles repeatedly invaded the country and even occupied Moscow. Alarmed by the threat of a Polish takeover, the General Assembly sought a Tsar who could rally the country's factions and preserve Russian independence. In 1613 the crown was offered to Mikhail Romanov, a prince whose family connection to Ivan's Anastasia gave him great respectability. Mikhail fought off the Poles, stabilized the government and established a dynasty that was to last three centuries, until the 1917 Revolution.

The early Romanovs presided over a period of social development and rapid economic growth, and at the end of the 17th century the dynasty gave Russia the Tsar seen as the architect of modern Russia: Peter the Great.

Like Ivan, Peter had a traumatic childhood surrounded by political intrigue. His father Alexis died when he was four, to be succeeded by one of Peter's half-brothers, the sickly Fyodor. On his death six years later, a power struggle resulted in Peter, then 10, sharing the throne with another half-brother, the feeble-minded Ivan: Ivan's sister Sophia ruled as regent.

Effectively excluded from government, Peter was frequently able to escape to the imperial estate outside

# 4

**Tsar Peter the Great, towering over his retinue in this 1907 painting, strides over the marshy site of his future capital and "window on the West", named St. Petersburg after his patron saint—today the city is known as Leningrad.**

near Moscow. At court, he hugely enjoyed telling coarse jokes that offended many of his listeners.

Peter saw that Russia was backward socially and technologically, and he determined to "open a window to the West" for progressive European ideas. Accordingly, he set forth in 1697 for an epoch-making tour of Europe.

Peter was travelling incognito, as "Seaman Peter Mikhailov". But this pose was less than successful, since the "seaman" had a retinue of about 250 people. His journey, which lasted for 18 months, took him to Germany, then down the Rhine River to Holland, where he lived and worked for three months as a carpenter in a shipyard, earning a shipbuilder's certificate. Elsewhere, he also studied anatomy, surgery and dentistry, explored museums and art galleries, and learnt how to cut up whale blubber. In England, he observed Parliament in session from the upper galleries.

The English government lodged him in a nobleman's house. This he left in such disarray—its furniture broken, its portraits used for target practice—that the owner submitted a large bill for damages. According to one story, Peter paid up by handing the man a huge uncut diamond wrapped in a piece of dirty paper.

Peter planned to visit Venice next, but his trip was cut short by news of a palace revolt. In his absence, conservative officers of the Streltsy Guard, fearful of his innovative ideas, sought to depose him. Peter rushed home in a fury, only to find that the uprising had already been put down, with hundreds of rebels killed and more than a thousand thrown in jail. But Peter was not satisfied. He ordered the prisoners to be roasted alive on a spit, one by one. As

Moscow. There he led a remarkably free existence, roaming the countryside by himself and wandering through the local village. By watching and helping, he acquired an astonishing set of skills. Although his talents may have been exaggerated in contemporary accounts, he could it was said build a stone house, cobble shoes, pull teeth, even cast a cannon.

According to one story, the young Peter came upon a sailing-boat in the imperial storehouse and was struck by its unusual design. Unlike the flat-bottomed craft that plied Russian rivers, this one was a round-bottomed boat, with a pointed prow and a keel. Peter put it in the water and found a

Dutch-born boatbuilder to teach him how to sail it. From this experience may have come Peter's lifelong love of boats and the sea, a passion that would eventually lead him to establish the Russian Navy.

In 1696, when Peter was 24, his half-brother died and Peter became sole ruler. By this time he was a giant of a man, 2.03 metres tall and of legendary strength. It was said that he could bend heavy silver plates as if they were paper and could fell a tree with an axe in seconds. His appetite for food and drink was gargantuan and he preferred to indulge it in the easy company of the foreign craftsmen—English, Scottish, Swiss and Danish—who lived each one neared death, his head was chopped off (Peter himself reputedly participated in this grisly finale). Then Peter had the heads impaled and placed throughout Moscow, to rot.

For all his barbaric behaviour, Peter continued to believe that Russia should be modernized. He began symbolically, compelling Russians to adopt the Western styles of dress he had observed in Europe. Men were ordered to shave their beards or else pay a tax; Peter even assisted in the shaving of some noblemen. Short coats were to be substituted for the long Russian kaftan; women were to shed their veils and attend parties in the tight-waisted, deeply cut gowns worn by French ladies.

His other reforms were more practical. He encouraged the construction of factories and founded schools of mathematics, navigation, astronomy, medicine, philosophy, geography and politics. He also started the first Russian newspaper, ordered the printing of 600 books and built a theatre in Moscow's Red Square.

He modernized the army to enable it to cope with continuing foreign invasions. After Russia lost 10,000 men and most of its artillery against a much smaller Swedish force in the Battle of Narva in 1700, Peter rebuilt his army in a single year. He instituted new standards of discipline, ordered training for battle rather than for parade-ground manoeuvres, and armed his troops with British-made flintlocks to replace the swords, lances and halberds they had previously carried. He even ordered church bells to be melted down to cast new artillery.

Eight years later, the Swedes, who had postponed further conquests of Russia while invading Poland and Saxony, returned. They moved into the Ukraine and there, in 1709, were destroyed in what is considered to be one of history's most critical encounters, the Battle of Poltava. Sweden was forced to give Russia its lands on the eastern shore of the Baltic—the European mainland—and the threat of Swedish domination of Northern Europe was permanently ended.

After this victory, Peter continued to refine his army; he also brought the Church under state control and reorganized the civil service, setting up 14 grades to which anyone could aspire. Even a peasant, properly schooled, could rise from the 14th grade to the first. Moreover, every civil servant above the 11th grade automatically gained the right to own land and serfs; above the eighth grade, such status became hereditary. Travelling this egalitarian route to advancement, Ilya Ulianov, son of a serf and father of the 20th-century revolutionary known as Lenin, managed to climb the ladder to the fourth grade and hereditary land entitlement. Thus Lenin himself was technically an aristocrat.

With the final victory over Sweden, Peter at last acquired his "window on the West", a safe, year-round route through the Baltic Sea to the rest of Europe. In expectation, he had already begun to build a port, the city now called Leningrad but originally named after Peter's patron saint, and thus in a way after Peter himself: St. Petersburg. It would seem to have been set on the worst possible spot—marshland at the mouth of the Neva River, where it flows into the Gulf of Finland.

Peter imported a multitude of French and Italian architects and artisans and proceeded at top speed. Tens of thousands of peasants, prisoners of war and army recruits were dragooned for labour. Often they dug with their hands, slept in the open and drank stagnant marsh water. So many died that the city was said to have been built on bones. In nine years, however, Peter had his great city—a metropolis of 34,500 buildings. He proclaimed it Russia's capital.

Peter's plan for his city included a network of canals, like those of Amsterdam, and broad, tree-lined streets. Houses were sized according to the status of their occupants. Common people were to have one-storey houses with four windows and a dormer; prosperous merchants, two-storey houses with dormers and a balcony.

Peter's own palace was a modest wooden building next to the naval headquarters, where he often took his meals, dining on rations of smoked beef and beer. However, his suburban Summer Palace on the banks of the Neva River, Petrodvoretz (also called Peterhof, a German name), was a 14-room mansion surrounded by elaborate gardens and spectacular fountains. Some of these waterworks catered to Peter's delight in practical jokes: "surprise" fountains sprayed water on the unwary when they happened to step on a particular stone.

It was at Petrodvoretz that the Tsar had a tragic confrontation with his only living son. Alexis had been born to Peter's first wife, a woman he never liked; eventually he banished her to a convent, in effect divorcing her. His second wife, with whom he lived for 23 years, was a commoner. They had 12 children, but only two survived childhood. Both were girls.

Alexis, the logical successor, was the pawn of conservatives who wanted to depose Peter. At Petrodvoretz, the Tsar accused his son of joining in a plot

# 4

against him. When Alexis answered equivocally, Peter had him imprisoned and "questioned" so severely that Alexis died. Peter himself died only seven years later, without ever having named a successor. His death was caused by an illness he contracted when he jumped into the icy water of the Gulf of Finland to help rescue a boatload of foundering sailors.

Peter's modernization was beneficial in many respects, but it also proved divisive. It created a Western-oriented gentry at odds with peasantry and clergy that violently resisted change from old Russian ways. Barely 40 years later, another strong leader widened this chasm. Catherine the Great at first welcomed liberal Western ideas and instituted reforms. By the middle of her reign, however, she reversed herself, setting Russia on a reactionary course that led, a century and a half later, to revolution.

Catherine was not even Russian, and "Catherine" was not her real name. She became ruler of Russia through a convoluted series of events set off when Peter the Great died with the imperial succession unsettled. The crown then passed among members of his family, coming to rest in 1741 on his daughter Elizabeth. Elizabeth named as her successor a nephew, a German prince, Peter of Holstein. She also selected a wife for Peter, a minor German princess, Sophie of Anhalt-Zerbst, who later adopted the appropriately Russian name of Catherine.

Clever and anxious to please, with a will of iron and energy to match, Catherine set out to learn her new language and to become an expert on everything Russian. She also soon ignored her husband, who drank heavily and was thoroughly disagreeable. In 1762, six months after his accession to the throne, Catherine engineered a coup that deposed him; then she had herself named Empress of Russia.

Eight days later Peter was conveniently killed, allegedly in a drunken brawl, probably at Catherine's instigation. "Little Mother, he is no more," a companion of his wrote to her. "Sovereign lady, the mischief is done."

The coup that eliminated Peter was carried out by a handsome young officer of the palace guards, Grigory Orlov, who was one of Catherine's many lovers. She was to have at least 21, and she never made much attempt to hide them. Catherine was not pretty, but she was witty and passionate, and she treated her favourites handsomely. One, Stanislaw Poniatowski, she made King of Poland.

Although Catherine craved power and worked hard to achieve it, she also enjoyed the trappings of majesty. For her coronation she ordered a crown containing almost 5,000 diamonds, 76 perfectly matched pearls and a 399-carat spinel that had once belonged to a Manchu Emperor of China. Thereafter the official headdress for all coronations, this crown was so heavy that one Tsar complained that wearing it gave him a headache.

She also spent millions of roubles on palaces and country estates, and she changed St. Petersburg from a city of wooden structures into an imposing one of granite. She enlarged and elaborated on Peter's city palace and next to it built a gallery, called the Hermitage, to house her library and art collection, filling it with the greatest masterpieces her agents could find—by Rembrandt, Raphael, Van Dyck and Rubens, among others. Ultimately, her collection contained some 4,000 paintings by Europe's finest artists.

This relentlessly intellectual woman, the possessor of a mind that she described as "more masculine than feminine", became fascinated with the ideas of the Enlightenment. This liberal philosophy, which was then sweeping Europe and America, held that human beings were basically good, rather than sinful (as Christian theologians have maintained). One of its fundamental principles held all people to be endowed with rights that no government could override.

Although such views hardly accorded with Russian tradition, Catherine carried on a brisk correspondence with such Enlightenment figures as Voltaire and Diderot. Diderot travelled to St. Petersburg to call on Catherine, but the visit did not go well. The Frenchman took liberties, tapping the Tsarina on the knee and calling her "my good woman". Catherine was not amused.

Under the influence of the Enlightenment, Catherine drew up a new code of laws, based on the premise that a monarch ruled not by the will of God but by the dictates of human reason—a significant difference. She also seemed ready to take up the Enlightenment principle of opposition to human bondage, which had persisted in Russia—even increased there—after it had declined in Europe.

By the 18th century, slavery was essentially gone in Western Europe, and serfdom, the medieval system that bound peasants to the land of a feudal lord, was about to disappear. But in Russia, serfdom expanded as tsars repaid favours with gifts of land—together with the peasants living on the land, who thus became serfs of the new landowner. By Catherine's time, approximately half the total population of

Russia were serfs, many of them living under conditions tantamount to slavery. One noblewoman in Catherine's court kept her hairdresser, who was a serf, in a cage so that he could not tell anyone that she was bald.

Any possibility that Catherine might free the serfs was foreclosed by an unexpected threat to her power: in the midst of a war with Turkey over the Crimea, Catherine was faced with a peasant rebellion in the Cossack homeland west of the Ural Mountains.

The uprising was led by a black-bearded Cossack named Pugachev, an army deserter who had persuaded other Cossacks to organize against the St. Petersburg government. Soon the Cossacks, fierce fighters who made up the mounted troops guarding the frontiers, were joined by other dissidents—serfs, miners, conservative monks and political exiles. Pugachev attracted some of his followers by claiming that he was the true Tsar, Catherine's late husband Peter, not dead after all. To convince doubters, he showed them the "Tsar's sign", a scar on his chest. Others he won over by promising them land of their own.

By 1773, Pugachev had attracted some 15,000 adherents, and he controlled large areas of eastern Russia. When he showed an inclination to move on Moscow, Catherine quickly concluded a peace with Turkey and sent part of her army to capture him. He was brought to Moscow in a cage, and there he was beheaded and quartered. In the months that followed, peasants from every village involved in the rebellion were hanged, and serfdom, far from being abolished, was extended. New laws made serfs of peasants then farming the rich lands of the Ukraine, where serfdom had been rare.

"The richest object that ever existed in Europe," Catherine the Great's jeweller said of the crown he made for her coronation. It holds 4,936 diamonds and a 399-carat spinel—which alone is worth "a load of golden ingots".

Though known for her extravagance, Catherine the Great was a hard-working Empress. She rose at five in the morning and spent 10 to 15 hours a day on state papers and legislation.

Catherine turned against the Enlightenment. She banned Voltaire's writings and attacked his ideas. As the years passed, she became more and more autocratic. But if her opinions changed, her lifestyle did not. To her legion of lovers she added the most remarkable of them all, the tall, dashing Grigory Potemkin, a well-educated guardsman 10 years her junior.

When he was introduced to her at a party at the home of her earlier lover, Orlov, Potemkin had the impudence to parody her German-accented Russian. The other guests were appalled, but Catherine laughed. A tempestuous love affair followed. Catherine delighted in Potemkin's knowledge of Greek

and Latin, French and German, and she showered him with endearments, calling him "my peacock", "my Cossack", "my golden pheasant". According to rumour, impossible to confirm, they were secretly married.

Although their ardour cooled after two years, Potemkin remained Catherine's closest friend and adviser; he selected all her subsequent lovers. He was rich in his own right, with luxurious tastes (he bathed in a silver bath and passed out diamonds to women at his dinner parties). Catherine made him richer. She presented him with several estates and built a magnificent palace for him in St. Petersburg.

Potemkin, for his part, served her well. He masterminded Russia's annexation of the Crimea in 1783, afterwards arranging for Catherine to make an impressive inspection trip through this area. As the guests floated down the Dnieper River on red and gold Roman galleys, he pointed out newly built, prosperous towns. This display of progress has been considered a fake, contrived to fool Catherine—giving rise to the expression "Potemkin villages", referring to any elaborate sham—but recent research has convinced many historians that the villages and the progress they represented were, in fact, genuine.

When Potemkin died of malaria in 1791, Catherine was desolated. She died five years later, leaving behind an enlarged country that was improved by her innovations—such as the enlightened code of law and her magnificent art collection—but divided and impoverished by her many extravagances.

Less than 20 years after Catherine's death, the country suffered the first of a series of disastrous events that were to plague it through the 19th century and

# CHRONOLOGY OF KEY EVENTS

**1000–700 B.C.** Along the northern shore of the Black Sea, a primitive farming culture flourishes among a Slavic people called Cimmerians. They herd animals, weave cloth and produce fine pottery.

**500 B.C.** Tribes of Slavic peoples from northern Europe live in the region stretching from the marshes of Poland east and south to the Don River.

**700–300 B.C.** The Scythians, nomadic horsemen from Central Asia, take control from the Cimmerians and Slavs and hold sway over grasslands from the Danube to the Don River and across the Caucasus Mountains into Asia Minor. Skilled metalworkers, the Scythians make lavish gold jewellery *(above)*, weapons and utensils.

**300 B.C.–200 A.D.** Iranian-speaking nomads, the Sarmatians, defeat the Scythians and establish the west-east trade route—reaching to the Baltic and Black Seas and beyond—that introduces Graeco-Iranian culture and eventually enriches Russia.

**200–370 A.D.** The Goths, Germanic invaders from the Baltic area, take over the Sarmatian domain, penetrating into the Crimea in 362.

**370–658** The Goths move on to other regions in Europe and Asia, pushed out by Asiatic invaders. These Eastern horsemen—including the Huns led by Attila and, later, the Avars—do not settle but sweep across the sparsely populated regions to the south.

**c. 658–900** The Khazars, a tribe of Asian traders, establish their rule in the lower Volga and the south-eastern Russian steppe. They build strong commercial ties with the Slavs to the north-west near the Baltic end of the trade route.

**862** The Varangians, led by Rurik the Viking, settle in Novgorod, in the northern part of Russia. One group is believed to have been called the Rus.

**882–912** Prince Oleg *(below)* moves southwards to seize control of Slavic communities from the Khazars and makes Kiev the capital of the first truly Russian state.

**980–1015** Vladimir, Grand Prince of Kiev, adopts the Christian faith of the Byzantine Church and establishes the Russian Orthodox Church.

**1019–1054** Kievan Russia reaches its zenith under Yaroslav the Wise, who promotes education, codifies law, supports the arts, builds cathedrals and cements alliances with foreign states. His death in 1054 ushers in a period of decline.

**1237–1240** The Tartars (or Mongols), already conquerors of much of Asia, sack Kiev in 1240 and inaugurate more than two centuries of control by Tartar overlords, or khans, ruling through Russian vassals.

**1240–1242** Alexander Nevsky, Prince of Novgorod, repels invasions from the north-west by Sweden and the Teutonic Knights.

**1328–1340** Ivan I, Prince of Moscow, expands his territory and becomes the Tartars' principal vassal. He arranges for Moscow to replace Kiev as the spiritual capital of Russia.

**1462–1505** Ivan III *(above)*—also known as Ivan the Great—renounces Tartar rule and establishes the independent Russian state. He is the first to assume the title of Tsar.

**1547–1560** Ivan IV—Ivan the Terrible—drives the Tartars from their remaining territories along the trade route to the Caspian Sea. He marries Anastasia Zakharina-Romanov, daughter of a powerful Russian family. Under her beneficent influence, he calls the first general assembly to advise him, orders the printing of books and builds St. Basil's Cathedral to commemorate the defeat of the Tartars.

**1560–1584** Anastasia Romanov mysteriously dies and Ivan IV turns to irrational repression. He sets up a secret security force, the *oprichniki (above)*, and, suspecting treason, razes Novgorod, killing thousands. In 1583, Cossack troops conquer Siberia, extending Russian rule into Asia.

**1598–1612** Boris Godunov, regent for Ivan's weak son, Fyodor, becomes Tsar; this begins the "Time of Troubles". Pretenders claiming to be Fyodor's murdered heir, Dmitri, seek the crown; one "false Dmitri", backed by Poland, rules briefly. The Poles occupy and burn Moscow in 1610.

**1612–1682** Prince Dmitri Pozharski, leading an army raised by a patriot, Kuzma Minin, drives the Poles from Moscow. A year later, the general assembly elects Mikhail Romanov Tsar, establishing the dynasty that rules until 1917. Mikhail's successors take the eastern Ukraine from Poland, and extend Russian influence in Siberia to the Pacific. Serfdom is established.

**1682–1725** Peter the Great *(symbolized by his axe, below, left)* becomes Tsar and attempts to modernize the country. He builds a navy, reorganizes the army and in 1697 tours Europe to gather Western ideas. Peter wages wars against Sweden, winning lands on the Baltic after the decisive Battle of Poltava in 1709. St. Petersburg is built and declared the capital.

**1762–1796** Catherine II—Catherine the Great—begins as a progressive and benevolent ruler but reverses liberalization after a vast peasant revolt in 1773. Her interference in the affairs of Poland leads to the partition of that country and to war with Turkey. Russia gains the Crimea, Lithuania and a large part of the Ukraine. Fur traders establish settlements in Alaska in 1784.

**1801–1812** Russia expands further, annexing Georgia and, in 1809, Finland. Scattered Russian settlements are established along the west coast of North America as far south as California; Tsar Alexander I orders forts to be built in Alaska. In 1812, Napoleon Bonaparte invades Russia and sacks Moscow *(below)*, but his army is repulsed and nearly annihilated. This victory makes Russia a leading power in Europe.

**1861–1876** Tsar Alexander II liberates the serfs *(above)*. Russia sells Alaska to the United States in 1867.

**1898–1903** The Social Democratic Party is formed and splits in 1903 into two factions: the moderate Mensheviks, and the extremist Bolsheviks led by Vladimir Ulianov, called Lenin.

**1904–1905** Russia occupies Manchuria and attempts to penetrate China and Korea, leading to the Russo–Japanese War and a humiliating defeat at the hands of the Japanese. Growing unrest spurs strikes and demonstrations; hundreds of men, women and children are killed on "Bloody Sunday", when police open fire on protesting workers. Yielding to pressure for reform, Tsar Nicholas II issues the October Manifesto, setting up the Duma, an elected assembly.

**1825–1856** Young army officers, calling for constitutional reforms and an end to serfdom, lead the Decembrist Revolt in St. Petersburg. The uprising is violently suppressed. Russia is defeated by Britain, France and Turkey in the Crimean War.

**1914–1917** Germany declares war on Russia. Major defeats lead Tsar Nicholas II to go to the front. Tsarina Alexandra is in charge in the capital. But the government is dominated by her adviser, the monk Grigory Rasputin, who is assassinated in 1916.

**1917–1918** Workers' strikes and a Moscow troop mutiny bring about the collapse of the monarchy. A provisional government is established under Alexander Kerensky. Political instability leads to the October Revolution: Bolsheviks, led by Lenin *(above, left)*, Leon Trotsky *(above, centre)*, Joseph Stalin *(above, right)* and others, seize power and in 1918 sign a peace treaty with Germany.

**1918** Civil war breaks out between the Bolsheviks and the anti-Communist White armies *(above)*. The Tsar and his family are executed.

**1920** The White Army is defeated and Lenin consolidates the power of the Communists.

**1922** Joseph Stalin *(top, left)* becomes General Secretary of the Communist Party, and the Union of Soviet Socialist Republics is officially established.

**1924–1929** Lenin dies, leading to a struggle for power between Stalin and Trotsky; Stalin wins and Trotsky is exiled. Intensive collectivization of farms and industrialization begin.

**1936–1938** Stalin undertakes the great purge. Millions of citizens whom he suspects of opposing him—including many scientists, artists and writers, as well as 200 of the country's top military commanders—are exiled or executed.

**1939–1945** The U.S.S.R. and Germany agree to carve up Poland between them, but in 1941 Germany invades the Soviet Union, reaching Moscow's suburbs. After huge losses of territory and lives—20 million killed—Soviet armies eventually defeat the German forces and go on to occupy much of Eastern Europe. As a result of the Yalta Conference, the U.S.S.R. gains control over Romania, Bulgaria, Poland, Hungary, Czechoslovakia, Yugoslavia, Albania and East Germany.

**1947–1950** The Cold War begins. A treaty of mutual assistance is concluded with the People's Republic of China. The U.S.S.R. successfully explodes its first atomic bomb.

**1953–1956** Stalin dies; Nikita Khrushchev *(below)* takes over, denounces Stalin and brings in some reforms. He crushes a revolt in Hungary.

**1957** An intercontinental ballistic missile is successfully tested and *Sputnik I*, the first space satellite, is launched.

**1960–1965** China and the Soviet Union spar openly, marking the start of the Sino–Soviet split. The Soviets launch the first manned space flight, leading to the first space walk *(above)*.

**1964–1965** Khrushchev is ousted, to be replaced by Leonid I. Brezhnev *(below)*. Efforts to revitalize industry give management more control.

**1968** The Soviet government sends troops into Czechoslovakia.

**1972** U.S. President Richard Nixon visits Moscow and signs the first Strategic Arms Limitation Treaty.

**1975** Soviets and Americans rendezvous in orbit for the first joint space exploratory mission, known as the *Apollo–Soyuz* Test Project.

**1979** The Soviets invade Afghanistan in an effort to crush an anti-Marxist Muslim rebellion. Fierce resistance by the Afghan guerrillas drains Soviet resources and manpower.

**1980** Interference in Poland suppresses liberal activities of Solidarity, the coalition of labour unions.

**1982** Leonid Brezhnev dies and is replaced by Yuri Andropov, former chief of the Soviet Committee for State Security—the KGB.

**1984** Yuri Andropov dies and is replaced by Konstantin Chernenko.

**1985** For the third time in 28 months, a Soviet leader dies: Mikhail Gorbachev (below) replaces Konstantin Chernenko. At a summit in Geneva, he and U.S. President Ronald Reagan agree to work for a 50 per cent cut in their strategic nuclear arsenals.

**1986** An explosion at Chernobyl nuclear power station in the Ukraine contaminates a vast area; 135,000 citizens are evacuated.

**1987** Gorbachev launches reforms to foster *perestroika*—"reconstruction"— and *glasnost*—"openness". He calls for greater democracy in the Soviet Communist Party and pardons 140 dissidents.

**1988** Mass demonstrations for independence are staged in Estonia, Lithuania and Georgia. At the United Nations, Gorbachev announces unilateral troop cuts of 500,000 men and calls for a "new world order" in international relations. His visit is cut short by an earthquake in Armenia (below) which kills 25,000.

**1989** The Soviet army withdraws from Afghanistan. In West Germany, in June, Gorbachev states that the Berlin Wall could one day disappear; five months later it becomes obsolete as the Soviet satellites in Eastern Europe begin to defect.

**1990** The Central Committee of the Soviet Communist Party adopts a resolution to surrender the party's 72-year-old exclusive right to rule.

into the 20th. Napoleon Bonaparte, representing the culture Catherine had once praised, invaded the country and occupied Moscow, although the severe Russian winter soon forced him to retreat. In December 1825, an even more ominous event took place. Liberal-minded army officers led soldiers to demonstrate in St. Petersburg for financial reforms, a constitutional monarchy and an end to serfdom. The Decembrist revolt, as it came to be called, was quickly snuffed out, and five leaders were hanged.

Many of the changes the reformers had asked for, including the abolition of serfdom, were made a generation later by a more moderate Tsar, Alexander II. But in 1881 Alexander was assassinated by a bomb thrown under his carriage by student revolutionaries (they had already made six previous attempts to kill him). Terrorist activity continued, and assassinations occurred with frightening frequency; in the single year of 1906, a total of 768 officials were killed.

The government was buffeted from within and without. In 1905, a humiliating defeat in a war with the small nation of Japan destroyed most of the antiquated Russian fleet. Then a workers' demonstration grew into a march by thousands of workers and their families to the Winter Palace. The Tsar, Nicholas II, a gentle but ineffectual man, was not at home. In his absence, his household troops opened fire on the crowd, killing some 500 men, women and children.

Bloody Sunday outraged the Russian people. Resentment flared against the Tsar himself, who, until then, had escaped direct blame for the country's troubles. An alarmed Nicholas hastily granted one of his people's demands:

he convened an elected assembly—the Duma—but it lacked any real power.

World War I proved to be the final disaster for the monarchy. The Romanov regime—a political anachronism, trying to run a 20th-century nation like an 18th-century agrarian state—was completely unprepared. Six weeks after Germany had declared war on Russia, the Russian generals were already complaining of a shortage of artillery ammunition, and were rationing some units to five shells a day. After mobilizing six million men, the government discovered it had only five million rifles.

In 1915, with Russian armies retreating everywhere and casualties in the millions, Nicholas left St. Petersburg to take personal command of the armed forces. In charge at home was Tsarina Alexandra, who relied on advice from am illiterate "holy man", Grigory Rasputin. Years before, he had allegedly stopped the haemorrhaging of the Tsar's haemophiliac son; ever since, his word had been law to the Tsarina, even though he was a coarse peasant, a drunk and a lecher. "My much loved, never to be forgotten teacher, saviour and instructor," she wrote to him, "my soul is only rested and at ease when you are near me."

Rasputin's influence was calamitous, and in December 1916 a group of noblemen decided to do away with him. But the monk was not easy to kill. First they fed him cream cakes laced with cyanide. When that had no effect, one of the assassins shot him. Rasputin dropped to the floor but then leaped up and tried to strangle his assailant. Finally, one of the conspirators pumped bullets into him until he fell, and the conspirators then made absolutely sure of his death by dumping

# 4

his body into the Neva River.

This tragic farce was but one of many such events presaging the collapse of the Empire. In February and early March of 1917, striking workers and citizens queuing for food filled the streets of the capital—which had now been renamed Petrograd. On March 11, soldiers at the Petrograd garrison mutinied and joined the workers in their protest; they set fire to police stations, burst into the jails and released the prisoners.

The Tsar's council of ministers hurriedly turned off the lights and slipped away from their meeting in the Admiralty building. Meanwhile, in the Tauride Palace on the other side of the city, the Duma formed a provisional government, and almost simultaneously, in the same building, the rioting workers and soldiers seized rooms and set up their own political action committee, the Petrograd Soviet.

Within days, Nicholas abdicated in favour of his brother Mikhail, who in turn relinquished the throne a day later. Thus, after 1,000 years, monarchy in Russia was over. Replacing it was a democracy so divided by factional infighting—among intellectuals, landholders, educated peasants and various shades of radicals in the Petrograd Soviet—that it was little better able to govern than the Romanovs.

Into this situation stepped a man destined to change Russia more profoundly than anyone since Peter the Great. Vladimir Lenin scarcely seemed cast for such a role. His father was a regional superintendent of schools, his mother a doctor's daughter, and he had a perfectly conventional upbringing. Though expelled from university for taking part in a student demonstration, Lenin was

never a firebrand until his brother was executed in 1887 for conspiring to assassinate Alexander III. He became a Marxist in 1891, was arrested in 1895, and was sent to Siberia.

On his release in 1900, Lenin left Russia and spent most of the next 17 years abroad, mainly in Switzerland, plotting revolution with the Bolsheviks, one of several radical groups.

Although the Bolsheviks participated in the popular uprisings that toppled the Romanov regime, Lenin himself was still in Switzerland. He got into the fray only with assistance from the German government, which, still at war with Russia, had a clear interest in furthering domestic unrest there.

The Germans agreed to transport Lenin and his party by rail across Germany and on to Stockholm; no one was to leave the railway carriage or communicate with anyone outside it. (The only person who did violate the pledge was the four-year-old son of one of the Russians, who stuck his head into the neighbouring carriage to ask, in French, "What does the conductor do?") They stopped briefly in Stockholm for Lenin to buy a pair of shoes, on the advice of a companion who said that a man in public life ought to look the part. But when it was suggested that he also buy an overcoat and some extra underwear, he balked, declaring that he was "not going to Petrograd to open a tailor's shop".

From Stockholm, the revolutionaries crossed the Swedish border into Finland on sleighs, then transferred to another train bound for the Russian capital. There, Lenin found a provisional government halfheartedly supported by the workers and soldiers of the Petrograd Soviet but dominated by intellectuals and prominent liberals.

Grigory Rasputin, the Siberian holy man who mesmerized Tsarina Alexandra and was a power behind the throne, sits with two women of the court. His baleful influence contributed to Nicholas' downfall.

He intended to unseat them, by using the Petrograd Soviet as his power base, and he managed to install Bolsheviks in leadership positions in the Soviet.

In the ensuing power struggle between the Bolsheviks and the provisional government, Lenin suffered a brief set-back when the Bolshevik party was outlawed and he had to flee to Finland. However, support for the provisional government dissipated rapidly and on the eve of November 7, 1917—October 25 by the old Julian calendar—the Soviet's rank-and-file members occupied all the principal government buildings and arrested the leaders of this provisional government. With this, the October Revolution, the Bolsheviks were in.

They took Russia out of World War I, as the Germans had hoped they would, but a civil war soon started in its stead. For the next three years, anti-Communist forces calling themselves the white armies—aided by 14 countries—fought the Communist Red Army for control of the country.

The fighting cost seven million lives—including those of the Tsar, his wife and his five children.

Although the Tsar had given up his rule over Russia, he had not fled the country, and he and his family were treated gently by the provisional government that initially took over. For five months the imperial family stayed at a summer palace south of Petrograd, but then angry mobs threatened the Romanov's safety and the provisional government sent them to Siberia—in a manner that was hardly typical of Siberian exile. The family travelled in a private railway carriage with a retinue of servants, including seven cooks, 10 footmen, six chambermaids two valets, a nurse, a doctor, a barber, a butler and a wine steward.

But soon after, the Bolsheviks seized power and the Civil War between the White and Red armies raged. In April 1918 it was rumoured that a White Army detachment might make an attempt to free Nicholas. The family was moved to a merchant's house in Ekaterinburg, now called Sverdlovsk, on the eastern slopes of the Ural Mountains. There, at two in the morning on July 17, the prisoners were woken, taken to the basement and shot with pistols. All were killed by the bullets except the Tsar's daughter Anastasia, who had to be finished off with bayonets. The bodies were taken to a nearby mine, where 200 litres of sulphuric acid and 400 litres of petrol removed all traces of the execution.

The Civil War dragged on until 1921, but by the end of 1920 the White forces—ill-equipped, outnumbered and lacking in popular support—had been defeated by the Red. By the time the fighting was over, Lenin had consolidated the Communist's power. He died of a stroke in 1924, and two key aides vied to succeed him. One was Leon Trotsky, a Jewish Ukrainian; the other was Joseph Stalin, a Georgian whom Lenin had admired for his "expropriations" of funds—bank robberies—to support the Bolsheviks in the days before the Revolution.

The two men differed in their ideologies. Trotsky believed, as had Lenin, that in order for Communism to succeed in Russia, it would have to be part of a world-wide overthrow of capitalism. Stalin, on the other hand, believed that Communism would have to be made to work in Russia before it could be exported around the world.

Stalin had a tremendous political advantage. In 1922, he had been made Secretary General of the Communist Party, and in that position had filled top government posts with his followers. By December 1927, Trotsky was out and Stalin had taken over. He was to become perhaps the most tyrannical figure in Russian history, heaping on his people repressions that rivalled those of Ivan the Terrible.

Ruthlessly, he set out to transform Russia into a world power by increasing its heavy industry with a series of Five-Year Plans. He also organized agriculture into collectives and state farms, overcoming the objections of many peasants with brutal dispossessions and numerous executions.

In the mid-1930s, believing that opposition to his policies was growing within the leadership, Stalin undertook what has since become known as the Great Purge. Virtually every remaining member of Lenin's original 1917 command group was arrested and tried, then exiled or executed; the same fate was dealt much of the Red Army officer corps, including more than 200 of the top 300 military commanders. In addition, the purge cut a wide swath through the secret police force, and it liquidated many economists, historians, engineers, scientists, musicians, artists and writers, as well as hundreds of foreign Communists who were in Moscow at the time. The true scale of Stalin's excesses can only be guessed at, but it seems clear that many millions of people were sent to the labour camps: most of them died there. Stalin even reached half way round the world to eliminate a rival. On August 20, 1940, Leon Trotsky, in exile in Mexico, was

A group of Bolsheviks, in and on an impounded car, keep an "enemy of the people" under surveillance. In the frenzied weeks following October 25, 1917, such revolutionaries rushed about the tsarist capital of Petrograd to wipe out opposition.

# 4

assassinated by an agent of Stalin who buried an ice axe in his skull.

The severest test for Stalin's leadership came during World War II. In 1939, Adolf Hitler struck a deal with Stalin, by which they would carve up Poland between them; but Hitler later turned on his ally of the moment and marched his troops into the Russian heartland. History was repeating itself, but this time the outcome was different. Instead of buckling under the German juggernaut, the Russians were strong enough to contain and then repel the German forces—thanks in part to Stalin's programme of rapid industrialization. Cost in life was dreadful: at least 20 million Soviet citizens killed.

Hitler was only the latest of the succession of foreign invaders who over the centuries had threatened Soviet security. The depredations of the Mongols, the Swedes and Napoleon's French forces, followed by the carnage of World War I, had left a legacy of wariness which World War II heightened into paranoia. The Soviet Union emerged from the war the strongest nation in Europe and Asia, rivalled in military might only by the United States, but the next few decades saw the Soviet Union adopt a policy of offensive defence, engaging in a relentless nuclear arms race with the West.

Aptly termed the "Cold War", the frosty relations between the Soviet Union and the West stopped short of outright conflict. But both the Soviets and the Americans developed unmanned nuclear missiles and nuclear submarines, and later multiple-warhead weapons and cruise missiles that targeted goals with uncanny accuracy. Simultaneously, the two nations competed for the mastery of space and the prestige it brought. The Soviets

scored a decisive win in 1957 when they launched *Sputnik 1*, the first man-made satellite; Western nations were astonished and fearful at the hitherto unsuspected scientific expertise to which *Sputnik* bore witness. The Americans, however, won the world's adulation in 1969 when they landed astronaut Neil Armstrong on the moon.

Back on earth, the Soviet motherland protected itself behind a chain of buffer states under Communist rule. Apart from Austria, all the Soviet Union's conquests in World War II, from Poland on the Baltic to Bulgaria on the Black Sea, became satellite states after 1945. Part of Germany fell within the Soviet sphere. Following a steady decline in relations between the Soviets and their former Western allies, the Iron Curtain—a term prophetically coined by former British Prime Minister Winston Churchill in 1946—literally took shape with the building in the early 1950s of fortifications snaking 1,393 kilometres through the heart of Germany. Nine years later, the erection of the Berlin Wall sealed the great East-West divide and increased the tension between the superpowers.

Eastern Europe bore the Soviet yoke unwillingly, but the Soviet leadership was ruthless in countering any signs of independence or insubordination. Red Army units crushed riots in East Germany in 1953 and stamped out a revolt in Hungary in 1956, killing at least 2,000 Hungarians. That tragedy left Eastern Europe subdued until, in 1968, the Czech party secretary Alexander Dubcek introduced tentative political and economic reforms in a move dubbed "the Prague Spring". A Russian-dominated Warsaw Pact army rolled into Czechoslovakia to put an end to the experiment, less brutally

than in Hungary in 1956 but just as effectively. Dubcek was replaced by officials appointed from the Soviet Union.

The start of the 1980s saw the first sign of a more compliant attitude in the Soviet Union towards its East European neighbours. Discontent in Poland had produced the Solidarity trade union which, though careful in its public utterances, ultimately sought a new political order. Partly for fear of economic retaliations from Western powers, the Soviet Union forbore to intervene when Solidarity organized a series of strikes in 1980.

But by then the Soviet Union was embroiled in its most disastrous foreign venture since World War II. In 1979, a Soviet army had invaded Afghanistan for the purpose of protecting a puppet regime against Afghan rebel forces. But what was planned as a short-term campaign became a drawn-out conflict of attrition against the passionately Muslim guerrillas, who saw themselves as warriors in a holy war against the infidel invaders. Realism only prevailed in 1989 when, after a decade of humiliation and frustration, the Soviet Union withdrew its 120,000 military personnel.

The withdrawal from Afghanistan was one of many indications of a more enlightened, progressive force within the Kremlin leadership. The new generation of politicians recognized fundamental defects in a superpower that led the world in space exploration and military might, yet could not adequately meet the needs of its own masses. They also saw that the huge military expenditures had not brought commensurate gains in security. It was time, they perceived, to restructure the Union and simultaneously to put it on a new footing in the world at large.

In Prague, during the 1968 invasion of
Czechoslovakia that followed the
Czech government's liberalizing
reforms, a young Czech defiantly
waves his national flag aboard a
Russian tank. Resistance was quickly
crushed by Moscow.

# THE LIVING CHURCH

After more than seven decades under an avowedly atheist government, the Russian landscape's most striking man-made features remain the onion domes of its Orthodox churches. More than 20,000 churches perform rites for crowds of worshippers much as they have over 10 centuries—although before the Revolution, Russia had nearly four times as many churches to serve half as many people.

Until the late 1980s, religious activity was actively discouraged by the state. Plain-clothes policemen often roughed up people attending Easter services; proselytizing was forbidden. Yet the Church not only endured but continued to thrive, tolerated by the government as a useful source of Russian unity, a role it played during World War II. As a result of this uneasy accommodation between state and church, the priesthood attracts well-educated applicants; congregations are growing; and the Orthodox Church increasingly glows with some glimmers of the richness of old.

In a traditional ritual, a mitred prelate conducts an Easter procession of monks around Trinity-Saint Sergei monastery in the complex of Zagorsk, 70 kilometres north of Moscow. With six churches and many chapels as well as a seminary, Zagorsk is the spiritual centre of Russian Orthodoxy.

An archbishop bearing a staff symbolizing his rank pauses to pet his dog on a walk through his diocese near Moscow. All appointments to church office—from monk to bishop—require government approval.

# ASCETICISM IN MONASTERY AND CONVENT

A monk in a monastery near Lvov in the Ukraine observes what the Church calls the discipline of prayer. There are six monasteries in the U.S.S.R., with membership in each limited to about 50. Monks, unlike parish priests, may not marry.

Monks learn manual skills such as welding *(right)* to increase their usefulness to the Church, but monasteries are now purely centres of religious study and no longer engage in commerce or community service.

A nun in her cell in the Convent of the Assumption at Piukhtitsy, Estonia, prays before her order's favoured icons. Piukhtitsy is one of 12 active convents, all devoted to ascetic contemplation and worship.

As part of their effort to be self-sufficient, nuns gather wild mushrooms to augment their food supply. They also produce religious accoutrements such as bishops' elaborate vestments.

Holding candles that symbolize Christ, a couple are married in an Orthodox ceremony after their civil marriage. Such supplementary weddings are increasingly popular.

In a church funeral, hymns are sung and prayers read as the dead lie in state. The printed prayers on the chests of the deceased will be placed in their folded hands before burial.

A newly baptized infant is given a symbolic tonsure as others await their turn. Although baptisms were politically inexpedient—recorded as derogatory notes in parents' dossiers—as many as half the children in some areas are baptized.

On the evening before Easter, a
church table is crowded with cakes,
cheeses and eggs brought to be
blessed before they are taken home
for the festive *razgovenie*, the meal
that breaks the Lenten fast. Easter
services draw such crowds that
admission is often by invitation only.

Despite a January temperature of
−20°C, parishioners surround an
outdoor altar to celebrate the
Epiphany at the 18th-century Church
of Saints Constantine and Helen in
Suzdal, east of Moscow.

Wearing the peasant costume he often
affected, the novelist and nobleman
Leo Tolstoy sits among trees on his
country estate. This photograph,
taken in 1908 when Tolstoy was 80,
is one of a series made for the Tsar by
a complex, three-exposure process.

# GIANTS OF IMAGINATION

The names themselves, heavy with their cargoes of *k's, y's* and *v's*, are at once familiar. When strung together, they suggest the colour and richness of the culture their owners helped to create: Tolstoy and Dostoevsky and Chekhov, Pasternak and Solzhenitsyn, Tchaikovsky and Rimsky-Korsakov and Stravinsky, Nijinsky and Pavlova and Diaghilev. And the towering works these great artists have produced—*War and Peace, Crime and Punishment, The Cherry Orchard, The Nutcracker, The Firebird*—possess a resonance, a strange power that sets them apart from the cultural achievements of other nations.

Like all great works of art, they have a universality that transcends time and place, but there is nonetheless something distinctly Russian about them (although many of their creators were not ethnic Russians but Siberians, Ukrainians or Georgians, amongst others). These creations evoke a spirit, or a tone, of the looming presence of the enormous land and its people. The physical and spiritual landscape that Leo Tolstoy evoked in *War and Peace*, written in the 1860s, has echoes in Boris Pasternak's 1957 novel *Doctor Zhivago*; it reverberates in the symphonies of Pyotr Tchaikovsky and the ballet music of Igor Stravinsky.

The presence of a distinctive national quality in the work of the best of these artists has certainly contributed both to the vitality of the country's culture and its tremendous popularity around the world—and at home. Soviet citizens are the world's leading cultural consumers. More books are published,

more film tickets sold, more theatres and opera houses and dance companies maintained in the Soviet Union than in any other nation. The debut of a new ballet or a public reading by a popular poet generates that unruly excitement that Western Europeans and Americans associate with championship sports competitions or rock concerts. The publication of a new book by a major author creates long queues outside bookshops—which are swiftly followed by a black market in hoarded copies when the edition runs out.

But perhaps the most remarkable aspect of this culture is its achievement of such greatness and popularity in an environment that was for so long hostile to individual creativity. During most of the last century and a half—the comparatively brief span in which virtually all of the great works were produced—all forms of art were subject to the dictatorial control of oppressive governments.

In the 19th century, the autocratic Romanov tsars tried to stifle any criticism of their regimes. From the late 1920s on, the Soviet rulers not only refused to allow criticism but also demanded that painters, writers and even musicians create works praising the state and its ideology. Stalin declared that artistic freedom was a bourgeois delusion; the purpose of art was to exalt the regime. After Stalin's death in 1953, his successors in the Kremlin occasionally tolerated creative independence, but until the advent of Gorbachev's *glasnost* in the 1980s these brief thaws were invariably

followed by new, harsh freezes.

Censorship under the tsars was not as fierce or efficient as it has been under Soviet governments. The tsarist watchdogs, according to this century's Russian-born (but self-exiled) novelist Vladimir Nabokov, were mostly "muddled old reactionaries that clustered around the shivering throne". They often had trouble spotting subversion if it was cloaked under even a thin disguise—and the artists quickly became adept in Aesopian language, that is, in disguising what they wished to say as fables and tall tales.

Russia's 19th-century artists also escaped some modern strictures: they might be forbidden to criticize the tsarist regimes, but they were not forced to praise them. Many of Russia's pioneering writers, composers and painters were "quite certain that they lived in a country of oppression and slavery", noted Nabokov, but they had "the immense advantage over their grandsons in modern Russia of not being compelled to say that there was no oppression and no slavery".

The artists of tsarist times had sufficient freedom to convey an astonishing amount of truth, and they did so first in literature, which exploded into new life in the early years of the 19th century. Western ideas and books, which had been flooding into the country since the 17th-century reign of Tsar Peter the Great, had caused tremendous intellectual ferment. Reacting to these ideas, writers created numbers of powerful works. Perhaps no other nation, in one century, has produced

# 5

**Alexander Pushkin won undying fame for his poetry—and notoriety for his card playing. The police kept a dossier on him that was headed, "No. 36, Pushkin, well-known gambler."**

more great novels, poems and plays.

The man who ignited the explosion was Alexander Pushkin, recognized as the nation's greatest poet. Born in Moscow in 1799, he grew up to be small, wiry, precociously clever and irresistible to women, with his exotically dusky skin—inherited from his great-grandfather, Ibrahim Hannibal, an Ethiopian prince who was adopted by the great Peter himself.

Pushkin published his first verse at the age of 15 and was famous before he was 20, both for his poetry and for his pursuit of titled women, ballerinas and prostitutes. He soon began keeping a list of his conquests, dividing them into two categories, "Platonic" and "Sexual". His wicked wit and magnetism made him the darling of St. Petersburg's drawing rooms, much like the fashionable young man he portrays in his great novel in verse, *Eugene Onegin*:

*His hair cut in the latest mode,*
*He dined, he danced, he fenced, he rode.*
*In French he could converse politely,*
*As well as write; and how he bowed!*
*In the mazurka, 'twas allowed,*
*No partner ever was so sprightly.*
*What more is asked? The world is warm*
*In praise of so much wit and charm.*

The world was warm, but the officials around Tsar Alexander I were anything but charmed by the poet: his womanizing involved him in duels and he gambled and drank to excess. Nor were they enamoured of his clever epigrams mocking church and state, or of the audacious *Ode to Liberty* that he wrote in Russian—in a magically pellucid, elegant way. He was hustled into exile in faraway Kishinev, a forlorn outpost in southern Russia.

But exile did not quiet Pushkin. He wrote more clever and subversive poems, gambled and drank with the Kishinev Army garrison, and flirted with the local women. He also took part in more duels. He arrived at one such dawn appointment—with a man whom he had accused of cheating at cards—nonchalantly munching some cherries. He popped one into his mouth just before the signal to fire. His adversary fired and missed. Pushkin, who had not deigned to shoot, dropped his pistol, spat the cherry stone in his enemy's direction and coolly strolled off.

The Tsar's officials eventually transferred their problem poet to Odessa to work in a government office, but then banished him to his family's estate near Pskov, west of St. Petersburg. There, Pushkin read voraciously, absorbed Russian folk tales told by his boyhood nurse and wrote prodigiously. So great is the power of Pushkin's best tales and poems that more than 20 operas—including the popular *Boris Godunov*—have been based on his works.

With the accession of a new Tsar, Nicholas I, in 1825, Pushkin was summoned back to the capital, where he became the Tsar's private and captive poet. The starchy and militaristic Tsar appointed him to various court positions but also insisted on personally overseeing his writing. The secret police kept tabs on his after-hours escapades. Pushkin continued to produce fine poetry and prose despite his imperial censor, and he resumed his rousing lifestyle, although his philandering was tempered by marriage in 1831 to a beautiful if vacuous 16-year-old (according to Pushkin, this was the 113th time he had fallen in love).

His bride, Natalya, was a dazzling addition to the court, and before long the Tsar himself was discreetly flirting with her while his poet quietly fumed. Pushkin was further humiliated when the Tsar made him a gentleman of the chamber, a post he could not refuse, primarily to ensure his wife's presence at court. Soon Natalya and a glamorous French baron named Georges-Charles d'Anthès began to spend an eyebrow-raising amount of time together. Pushkin continued to fume but did nothing until he received anonymous letters mocking him as a cuckold. Suspicion has since arisen that government officials, perceiving a stratagem that might rid them of the obstreperous poet, arranged for the letters to be sent. This insult spurred Pushkin to challenge d'Anthès. The French baron's bullet struck Pushkin in the upper thigh, shattering the bone. After two days of agony Pushkin died, aged 37, while by his bed his wife blubbered, "Forgive me! Forgive me!"

His death prompted an outpouring of public grief; more than 30,000 people filed past his casket in a single day. Notables and newspapers eulogized the poet, but the most moving tribute was offered by an elderly citizen seen weeping bitterly by the coffin. Asked if

Fifty fountains grace the formal
gardens of the huge Summer Palace
that Peter the Great built in St.
Petersburg, now Leningrad. The
gardens and the palace are Western in
conception, not Russian; the
architects were French and Italian.

he had known Pushkin, the man replied: "No, but I am a Russian."

Pushkin set the stage for the great writers that would follow, especially in one of his last works, a long poem called *The Bronze Horseman*. His themes—the conflict between the individual and the state, the powerlessness of frail humans in the face of the forces of nature, the dangerous irrational depths within all human beings—preoccupied his two immediate successors, the poet Mikhail Lermontov and the playwright and novelist Nikolai Gogol. Lermontov—who was shot dead in a duel at the age of 26 in 1841—wrote outspoken political verses attacking the hypocrisy and stupidity of the ruling class. He produced subjective poems that prefigure the psychological probings of later writers. In *The Demon* he imagines a malign figure who proclaims:

*I am he, whose gaze destroys hope,*
*As soon as hope blooms;*
*I am he, whom nobody loves,*
*And everything that lives curses.*

And he dwelled on the Russians' ambivalent but stubborn love for their land. In a brief poem, "My Country", Lermontov opens with: "I love my country, but that love is odd: My reason has no part in it at all!" and continues:

*Ask me not why I love, but love I must*
*Her fields' cold silences,*
*Her sombre forests swaying in a gust,*
*Her rivers at the flood like seas.*

Gogol loved his country equally, or said he did. He was a political conservative and a defender of the tsarist autocracy. But when he wrote, his fantastic imagination created a nightmare land, a sprawling, ugly, ramshackle

# 5

One of the magnificent Easter eggs made by Russia's greatest jeweller, Carl Fabergé, holds a dozen tiny views of royal residences in a quartz globe adorned with diamonds, enamel and gold. Starting in 1884, the French-descended Fabergé did more than 50 of these *objets d'art*— masterpieces of imagination and craftsmanship—for the imperial family. This one was a gift from Nicholas II to his wife in 1896.

place peopled by grotesques. His satiric play *The Inspector General* presents a hilariously inept group of petty officials in a provincial town. The mayor, Gogol says, is "a grafter" adept at quick switches from "servility to arrogance"; the judge, who also takes bribes, "wheezes and huffs like an antique clock that hisses before it strikes the hour"; the postmaster opens everybody's post; the Director of Charities neglects his patients— "stick some clean gowns on the patients," the mayor tells him. "I don't want them looking like chimney sweeps"—and the teachers and policemen are lunatics or drunks, or both.

But *The Inspector General* is outdone by Gogol's great (and only) novel, *Dead Souls* (finished in 1842), which offers an unmatched rogues' gallery of bizarre creatures. The plot is itself a mordant Gogolian joke. A swindler named Chichikov travels the countryside, buying dead serfs (or "souls") from provincial landlords and, armed with the papers proving his ownership of these deceased workers, sells them to unsuspecting buyers as if they were alive. In the course of his dealings, Chichikov encounters what seems to be the entire rural population—landlords, innkeepers, serfs, coachmen, petty officials. Everyone is misshapen, physically and spiritually, in some way.

Among the writers whose genius dominated the latter half of the century—Turgenev, Tolstoy and Dostoevsky—it was Fyodor Dostoevsky who most revered Gogol. His work also gives sombre pictures of the country, lit by fantastic comedy. The shy, epileptic son of a not-very-successful and evidently foul-tempered physician, Dostoevsky received the first of the shocks that marred his life when his father was

murdered by an enraged coachman. Whether or not the young Dostoevsky had wished, consciously or subconsciously, for his abusive father's death, patricide was a dominant theme in his novel *The Brothers Karamazov*, and he was fascinated all his life by violent crime and the criminal mentality.

His family was impoverished by the father's death, and Dostoevsky felt himself among the downtrodden. His sympathy for society's victims led him to join a group of young radicals that was ferreted out in short order by the tsarist police. Dostoevsky and 20 others were tried and sentenced to death. Three days before Christmas in 1849, the conspirators were dressed in white shrouds and brought before a firing squad, but at the last minute the execution was halted on orders from the Tsar; one man was led away insane. Dostoevsky was banished to Siberia for four years' hard labour and several years of army service. Eventually pardoned by Tsar Alexander II, he chronicled his prison experiences in *House of the Dead*, the first of the scarifying accounts of Russian prison camps that ever since have continued to appear— as in Alexander Solzhenitsyn's *One Day in the Life of Ivan Denisovitch*.

His experiences did not make Dostoevsky a confirmed revolutionary. Rather, he turned to Slavophilism, a belief that only in Russia and her Slavic peoples, and in the Christianity of the Orthodox Church, was there salvation from the corrupting influence of Western materialist ideas.

Dostoevsky's views coalesced in the first great novel he wrote after his return from Siberia, *Crime and Punishment*. The hero, who is also the villain, is an impoverished student named Raskolnikov. He commits a hideous crime, splitting the skulls of an elderly woman moneylender and her sister with a hatchet. Robbery is one motive, but another is drawn from Raskolnikov's reading of German philosophers who seemed to preach that a "superior" man had the right to crush lesser humans on his path to greatness.

Raskolnikov has hardly committed the murder, however, before being overwhelmed by feelings of guilt. He is "seized with panic", Dostoevsky writes, "not because of any fear for himself, but in sheer horror and disgust at what he had done". Back in his own room, he falls into a stupor, awakening only to recall the grisly murder scene and to be assailed by "the conviction that everything, even his memory, even plain common sense, was abandoning him." "'What if,' Raskolnikov thinks in his near-delirium, 'it is already beginning, if my punishment is already beginning? Yes, yes, that is so!'"

Remorse drives Raskolnikov to commit one subconscious blunder after another, to follow a path of irrational behaviour that inevitably reveals his guilt to the police. Convicted and sent to Siberia, he achieves salvation—explains Dostoevsky in an almost apocalyptic ending—through suffering, humility, the Bible and a new-found ability to love his fellows. "Life had taken the place of dialetics," Dostoevsky writes, heralding "the gradual rebirth of a man," his "gradual passing from one world to another."

Dostoevsky wrote *Crime and Punishment* in little more than a year. Like his hero, he was tormented by debt. A literary magazine he had been running collapsed. Then his brother died, and Dostoevsky had to support the widow and children. Worst of all, he was a compulsive gambler, often losing at

## VENERATED RELICS OF MUSCOVITE ART

**This 12th-century icon of Christ, done in Novgorod, shows the Byzantine influence.**

Among the greatest of the treasures to be found in Russia are the thousands of icons—religious subjects painted on wood panels—that were produced by anonymous artists in monasteries and church-sponsored workshops from the 11th century through to the 17th century. These paintings not only portrayed Christ, the Virgin, saints and angels, but were also holy objects themselves, to be prayed to and venerated. Icons hung in every church and family household; many of them were credited with miraculous powers to cure the sick or repel foreign invaders.

Because icons were holy, they were not meant to be realistic. They were two-dimensional, lacking the illusion of depth that Renaissance artists in the West were pursuing at that time. Nor did any of the icon painters strive for originality. Rather, icons were patterned after time-honoured designs laid down in a handbook, called the *Podlinnik*.

The artists were given the freedom, however, to experiment with their colours. Their brilliant hues, combined with strong and simple designs, make the finest of these holy images powerful works of art as well as eloquent testimony to the deep Christian faith of Old Russia.

# 5

roulette every rouble he possessed. But slowly, with enormous effort, he wrote his way out of debt. *Crime and Punishment* was a success, and he followed it with a novel about a simpleminded Christian saint, called *The Idiot*. This was followed by the works some critics consider his masterpieces, *The Possessed* and *The Brothers Karamazov*.

The title of *The Possessed* is sometimes translated as *The Devils*. The devils in question are a group of would-be revolutionaries whose goal is a materialist Russia free of all moral restraints. In a devastating vision of this new political state and its amoral freedom, Dostoevsky prefigures the 20th-century totalitarian regimes. "I'm afraid I got rather muddled up in my own data," one revolutionary says, "and my conclusion is in direct contradiction to the original idea with which I started. Starting from unlimited freedom, I

arrived at unlimited despotism."

Another describes this despotism: "Every member of the society spies on the others, and he is obliged to inform against them. Everyone belongs to all the others, and all belong to everyone. All are slaves and equals in slavery." Creative genius, disruptive of totalitarian order, was to be eradicated: "A Cicero will have his tongue cut out, Copernicus will have his eyes gouged out, a Shakespeare will be stoned." The only thing the new state will want "is obedience. The only thing that's wanting in the world is obedience."

One character in the book, Shatov, seems to speak for Dostoevsky. "I believe in Russia," he says. "I believe in the Orthodox Church. I—I believe in the body of Christ—I believe that the Second Coming will be in Russia."

After immersion in Dostoevsky's dark and tormented world, it is like

Fancifully decorated window frames like these adorn many of Siberia's wooden houses. This traditional folk art includes intricate fretwork often enlivened by stylized birds and flowers *(opposite page, centre)*.

emerging into the sunlight to read the works of Tolstoy. Not that violence and anguish have no place in his novels. In *War and Peace* he describes Napoleon's 1812 invasion of Russia in gory detail; his other long novel, *Anna Karenina*, ends with the heroine, Anna, throwing herself under a train. His characters are mostly quite sane, and his heroes are eminently so; they play out their dramas for the most part in daylight and in the open countryside. In contrast to Dostoevsky's fevered writing, Tolstoy's prose is clear, leisurely and as naturally paced as a heartbeat.

In origin the two writers were as different as their works, yet they arrived at very similar conclusions about humanity's need for spiritual regeneration through the teachings of Christ. Tolstoy was born in 1828 to aristocratic privilege, heir of a count, on his family's

1,600-hectare estate at Yasnaya Polyana, 200 kilometres south of Moscow. Singularly gifted and energetic, he forged a career that brimmed with contradictions: he was an officer's son and an officer himself, who chronicled war but later embraced pacifism, a nobleman who habitually wore peasant garb, a sophisticate who preferred the bucolic life of the countryside, a great writer who eventually renounced literature. In his youth he gambled and caroused in St. Petersburg but then, disgusted with his profligacy, he fled for the Caucasus Mountains. Shortly afterwards, Tolstoy served in the Crimean War, and his account of the siege of Sevastopol helped to establish his reputation as a promising author.

Literature then, as later, did not command Tolstoy's entire attention. He returned to the family estate and, always concerned for the welfare of its

# 5

workers, started a special school for the peasant children, and himself served as the principal teacher. He also did heavy labour in the fields.

Tolstoy added to this taxing regime the writing of *War and Peace*. The novel, published between 1865 and 1869 in six volumes, is most remarkable perhaps for its inclusiveness. All human life seems to be here, from what one character, Prince Andrei, calls the "best human attributes—love, poetry, tenderness", to the brutalities of war on a vast scale. Birth, marriage and familial love are included, along with unfulfilled hopes, heartbreak and death. Tolstoy took pains to give each of his characters a distinctive personality and voice; one critic noted that even the book's dogs are individualized. Tolstoy's characterizations are deft. Introducing an aristocrat who is a master of vacuous chitchat, Tolstoy has him say an insincere compliment and then adds, "like a wound-up clock, by force of habit [he] said things he did not even wish to be believed".

Even the completion of his huge masterpiece left Tolstoy feeling unfulfilled. He resumed teaching, brooded about religion and hurled himself into the simple satisfactions of physical labour. "I work, chop, spade, mow and do not give one thought to literature and those awful literary folk," he wrote to a friend. But soon he was working on the lengthy portrayal of the Russian upper crust that became *Anna Karenina*. Dostoevsky, a friend reported, was so excited by the book that he ran around St. Petersburg, "waving his hands and calling Tolstoy the god of art". But the god of art himself soon soured on his own creation; his religious ruminations convinced him that all art was ungodly because it was based on imagination—

that is to say, deceit—and he called even his own *Anna* "an abomination that no longer exists for me".

In his last three decades Tolstoy embarked on a search for a mystical inner truth—*istina* in Russian—rather in the manner of one of Dostoevsky's redeemed sinners. He became something of a holy man to whom others made pilgrimages and, protected from official persecution by his worldwide fame, he became a savage critic both of the government and of the Orthodox Church. He swore off meat, wine, hunting and smoking, advocated non-violent resistance to authority and developed his own quirky brand of Christianity. He was still following his own quixotic impulses when he died of pneumonia in 1910 at the age of 82. He had fled from a discordant marriage to join a band of his religious followers in the Caucasus, where he was stricken at a village railway station. His last words were fittingly Tolstoyan: "The truth ... I love man ... How are they ... "

Like Pushkin and Tolstoy, their celebrated contemporary Ivan Turgenev was born to wealth: his family at one time owned as many as 5,000 serfs, including musicians that formed an orchestra; the sole duty of some serfs was to feed the Turgenev pigeons. As a young novelist he assailed the institution of serfdom and had the satisfaction of contributing to its abolition in 1861, but he paid the price—a brief jail term and two years' house arrest.

Turgenev was an ardent admirer of Western culture—especially the technical virtuosity of the French novelist Gustave Flaubert—and his works lack the intensity found in the novels of Tolstoy and Dostoevsky. But few writers ever more gracefully described the Russian countryside. In *Fathers and*

The implacable hostility of Stalin and his successors to all modern art has obscured the fact that for a brief, heady period between 1910 and 1930, Russian painters and sculptors were by far the most daring of the avant-garde. A few of these artists—notably Vasily Kandinsky and Marc Chagall—fled Soviet orthodoxy to win fame in the West, but they were only part of an astonishingly productive group, now almost forgotten, who pioneered modern art.

Many of the Russians studied in Paris and other hotbeds of experimental art before World War I and brought home the inspiration of Picasso, Matisse and others. But they then carried experimental forms to new extremes, with innovations that only later appeared in the West. Under the banners of several "isms", Rayonism, Constructivism, Suprematism, such painters as Kazimir Malevich and Mikhail Matiushin *(right, above)* did away with all realistic elements and created pure abstractions—geometric arrangements of line and colour—with such titles as "Red Square in Black" and "Counter Relief".

For a brief period after the political revolution of 1917 this art won government approval, and a number of artists, among them El Lissitzky *(right)*, devoted their talents to the new Soviet state. But the Kremlin gradually turned against their abstract modes, and in the early 1930s Stalin completed the destruction of the avant-garde by decreeing that all art must be "comprehensible to the millions"; the only mode allowed became a mawkish representational style, "Socialist Realism" *(far right)*.

# RISE AND FALL OF A PRECOCIOUS, DARING AVANT-GARDE

Bands of luminous colours flash across an abstract painting entitled "Movement in Space", done in 1918 by the musician and artist Mikhail Matiushin. It prefigured by 40 years the work of the schools of Abstract Expressionist painting after World War II. Matiushin's music was equally unconventional: one piece included cannon shots and the sounds of a crashing aeroplane.

A 1919 political poster of geometric forms by El Lissitzky, "Beat the Whites with the Red Wedge", exhorts the Communist Red Army to defeat its Civil War enemy, the White forces.

In sharp contrast to the fresh work of the avant-garde is this trite Socialist Realist painting by Efim Cheptsov, in which a uniformed party worker addresses villagers in a local theatre.

*Sons*, he offers a vision of a country evening: "The sun had hid behind a small aspen grove" that spread its shadow "across the still fields. A peasant could be seen riding at a trot on a white horse along a dark narrow path skirting that distant grove" as the "setting sun flushed the trunks of the aspen trees with such a warm glow that they seemed the colour of pine trunks."

The last of the great 19th-century writers, Anton Chekhov, was the grandson of a serf, born in 1860 in the city of Taganrog. He worked his way through school, then supported his family by scribbling comic sketches for newspapers and magazines while studying medicine in Moscow.

But these difficult years did not embitter Chekhov. He became the most cheerful and sociable of men—ready always, noted a friend, "to sing with the singers and to get drunk with the drunkards". He was devotedly public-spirited, and worked long hours as a physician in Moscow's poor suburbs, mostly without pay; during a cholera epidemic he alone cared for the sick in 25 villages; he built four schools for peasant children entirely with his own funds; he made an exhausting trip to a tsarist prison colony on the Pacific island of Sakhalin and wrote an account of life there, simply because he felt it his civic duty to investigate prison conditions. Even after he contracted the tuberculosis that would kill him at 44, he was not deflected from his concern for people around him. He wrote to a friend, "If every man did what he could on his little bit of soil, how marvellous our world would be!"

Despite all his activities, he managed to create what a critic called "that colossal, encyclopaedically detailed Russian world of the 1880s and 1890s which goes by the name of *Chekhov's Short Stories*." These narratives advance no political theories but portray the lives of the people: peasants and intellectuals, aristocrats and clerks, landowners and the hopelessly poor. The stories are sometimes humorous, but the humour is mixed with sadness. In one, "In the Ravine", a peasant comforts a woman whose baby has died: "'Never mind,' he repeated. 'Yours is not the worst of sorrows. Life is long, there is good and bad yet to come, there is everything to come. Great is Mother Russia.'"

This melancholy also suffuses Chekhov's plays, which portray idealistic intellectuals unable to translate their ideals into action. In *The Three Sisters*, a trio of sensitive provincial women resolve to go to Moscow—to achieve something, perhaps, or at least to see some of life—but they never leave their crumbling country estate. In *Uncle Vanya*, a frustrated idealist tries twice to shoot the man he believes responsible for his wasted life—and misses. In *The Cherry Orchard*, an impoverished family is powerless to prevent the forced sale of part of their property; the last sound in the play is of axes chopping down their beloved orchard. Sonya, the heroine of *Uncle Vanya*, speaks for all Chekhov characters: "There is nothing for it. We shall live through a long chain of days and weary evenings; we shall patiently bear the trials which fate sends us." And she adds: "When our time comes we shall die without a murmur."

The richness of the golden age of Russian literature was equalled in the performing arts of the 19th and early 20th centuries. In music and dance, creative geniuses in Russia set world standards. And like the writers of their time, they imbued their works with quintessentially Russian intensity.

During the years when Tolstoy, Dostoevsky and Turgenev were writing, Pyotr Tchaikovsky was composing his brooding, romantic symphonies, and a group of gifted amateurs known as the "Mighty Handful" were joining him in lifting Russian music to a new height. The composers, like the writers, drew on peasant folklore, and they filled their scores with the same spaciousness and gentle rhythms that Turgenev and other writers employed to evoke the land. The musical outpouring included symphonies and operas as well as compositions that helped to make Russian ballet pre-eminent.

The most prominent members of the Mighty Handful were Aleksandr Borodin, Modest Mussorgsky and Nikolai Rimsky-Korsakov, bound together by a common lack of classical musical training and the fact that all three of them had other, non-musical careers: Borodin was a professor of chemistry, Mussorgsky was a government official and Rimsky-Korsakov was a naval officer. For a time Mussorgsky and Rimsky-Korsakov shared a St. Petersburg flat furnished with a piano and a table. Mussorgsky used the piano in the morning while Rimsky-Korsakov wrote at the table; in the afternoon Rimsky-Korsakov took over the piano while Mussorgsky went to his office.

Borodin, the illegitimate son of a Georgian prince, taught himself to play the violin and cello and composed his first concerto when he was 13. After studying in Western Europe for four years and gaining his chemistry degree, he returned to St. Petersburg and began composing in his spare time. He eventually produced two symphonies and the unfinished opera *Prince*

*Igor*, which Rimsky-Korsakov completed after Borodin died in 1887. The opera's "Polovtsian Dance" segment, redolent of Russia's Asiatic East, is perhaps his best-known legacy.

Mussorgsky, musically the most radical member of the group, tried to reproduce the sounds of nature and the Russian speech in his often non-melodic compositions. *Night on the Bare Mountain*, written in 11 days, was an explosive depiction of a Ukrainian witches'-Sabbath ceremony. The 1874 production of his opera *Boris Godunov* was both the culmination of his career and the beginning of his sad, alcoholic decline. He was devastated when the opera was dropped after only 20 performances and—cursed by an unstable, self-destructive personality—drank himself to death by the age of 42.

Rimsky-Korsakov was the youngest and most prolific of the three. Son of a provincial governor, he became a naval officer and spent three years sailing the world with the Imperial Fleet. His musical talent was recognized by the court and he was given a professorship at the St. Petersburg conservatoire, followed by a special assignment as inspector of naval bands. These appointments freed him to compose. In 15 operas and numerous symphonic pieces, such as the popular *Scheherazade* suite, Rimsky-Korsakov drew his inspiration and melodies directly from Russian folk music; he once followed a servant round a house "to catch a tricky rhythm" in a tune she was singing. In later years he was world-famous as a composer and conductor, becoming director of the Imperial Russian Symphony and the lone foreign member of the French Academy.

Looming above these three was the unique and majestic figure of Pyotr

A muscular young ballet student practises classic movements in one of Moscow's many dance schools. So great is the Russian passion for ballet that there are 40 major dance companies flourishing in the nation.

Ilyich Tchaikovsky, the greatest composer of the golden age. Trained as a lawyer, he then turned to music in his twenties, persisting in spite of critical disparagement so severe that he burnt some of his scores in despair. Gaining prominence with his symphony *Winter Dreams* in 1868, he went on to produce a magnificent repertoire of symphonies, operas such as *Eugene Onegin*, and the classic ballets *Swan Lake*, *The Nutcracker* and *The Sleeping Beauty*. Ballet had been popular in Russia for several years—Pushkin had called it "soul-inspired flight"—but Tchaikovsky's collaboration with the French-born Marius Petipa, director of the imperial ballet, culminated Petipa's long campaign to elevate Russian dance to international supremacy.

Tchaikovsky rejected the nationalism of the Mighty Handful; his aim was to compose music that "explored the human soul". His choice of Shakespeare's *Romeo and Juliet* as the subject of an opera is characteristic: "There are no Tsars," he said, "no marches, there is nothing that constitutes the routine

of an opera. There is only love, love and love." The music in his six symphonies, alternately joyful and intensely melancholy, joins a distinctive Russian sensibility to a humanity that transcends political borders.

By the time Tchaikovsky died, in 1893, Russian literature, music and dance were universally recognized as world treasures. In the ensuing three decades of political ferment, Russians would lead the way in new art forms such as film and abstract painting, while a new generation of writers and composers revitalized literature and music with exciting experimentation.

The era that began in the 1890s and ended with Stalin's crackdown in the early 1930s was a time of growth. By the eve of the Revolution, there were 6,000 newspapers and magazines published in Moscow and St. Petersburg alone. A hundred poets earned their living with their pens. The theatrical genius Konstantin Stanislavsky introduced a new and much-emulated acting technique—"the Method"—at his innovative Moscow Art Theatre. The Russian ballet, with Stravinsky's music and inspired choreography by Sergei Diaghilev, became clearly the best in the world, exporting spectacular productions starring such virtuoso dancers as Anna Pavlova and Waslaw Nijinsky. (Nijinsky's leaps were so prodigous that sceptics checked his shoes for rubber and the stage for mechanical aids; the dancer explained disingenuously that the trick was "to go up and then pause a little up there".)

The heavy hand of Stalinist conformity brought an end to this effervescent time. Successive governments strictly monitored all the arts, chiefly through the various national unions to which writers, composers and other

# 5

artists were required to belong. Established when Stalin was consolidating his power in the early 1930s, the unions spelt out the artist's role as political cheerleader. The Union of Soviet Writers defined its goal as "the creation of works" that would be "saturated with the heroic struggles of the world proletariat" and would "reflect the great wisdom and heroism of the Communist Party". Similar standards were enunciated by the unions of musicians and painters. The works that adhered to these prescriptions—novels extolling construction projects, heroic portraits of party leaders—won little recognition outside the U.S.S.R.

The Writers' Union enforced its policies because of its ownership of book-publishing houses and literary magazines. It prevented the appearance of any material diverging from the party line, and it was able to keep non-members from earning their livelihood. Joseph Brodsky, a dissident poet who did not belong to the union, was prosecuted for continuing to write poetry. A judge ordered him to produce "documentary evidence" that he had the right to compose verse, then ruled that he was a "parasite" and sentenced him to five years' hard labour. He was eventually forced to emigrate.

Despite such persecution and omnipresent censorship, some 20th-century writers managed to say what they wanted to, and produced works that rival those of their great predecessors. The popular poets, who drew thousands to their public readings, were generally circumspect on stage, but they too could provide a tangy note of non-conformity. Of these poets, the best known in the West, Yevgeny Yevtushenko, drifted in and out of official favour as his verses nudged the limits of governmental tolerance.

Other writers, such as the acclaimed poet Anna Akhmatova, took even greater risks and often suffered for it. Akhmatova's first husband was killed, and her third husband and her son were imprisoned in labour camps. She was barred from publishing her work and expelled from the Writers' Union. Still, in lines that were eventually heard, she expressed the anguish of the artist in chains:

*For some the wind can freshly blow,*
*For some the sunlight fade at ease,*
*But we, made partners in our dread,*
*Hear but the grating of the keys,*
*And heavy-booted soldiers' tread.*

Another of the more courageous was Boris Pasternak, whose refusal to praise the party in conventional verse made his life a perilous transit of the minefields of Soviet officialdom. For most of his career Pasternak was a lyric poet with a gift for evoking nature and an intensely personal style. By 1934 he had attained such stature that Stalin telephoned one day to ask his opinion of the works of the dissident poet Osip Mandelstam. Pasternak praised Mandelstam highly and tried to change the subject. He wanted to have a long talk with the supreme leader, he said later, "about love, about life, about death", but Stalin cut the conversation short.

Two years afterwards Pasternak "confessed" at a writers' congress that his temperament was incompatible with "socialist realism". Censured as a result, he was prevented from publishing his work for the next seven years. He probably would have suffered worse punishment had not a friend been head of the Writers' Union.

In the mid-1940s, Pasternak began a novel, *Doctor Zhivago*. "In it I want to convey the historical image of Russia over the past 45 years," he wrote. "It is literature in a deeper sense than anything I have ever done." When he finished the book, he was not allowed to publish it. He smuggled the manuscript to Italy, and the novel appeared to international acclaim in 1957.

*Doctor Zhivago* won a Nobel prize for Pasternak, but the government made him decline it and he was reviled as a counterrevolutionary demon. The two years that remained before he died at

**Muscovites throng a freely organized exhibition of modern paintings. Until the cultural thaw under *glasnost* in the late 1980s, such displays needed official permission; one avant-garde show was crushed by police bulldozers.**

70 in 1960 were clouded by harassment and forced isolation.

More than a quarter of a century was to pass before *Doctor Zhivago* was published in the Soviet Union. It was an immediate bestseller. By then, however, Mikhail Gorbachev's liberation of the arts meant that infinitely more controversial works were appearing. The first literary sensation under *glasnost* came in 1986: Chingis Aitmatov's *The Place of the Skull*, a searing attack on drugs, the destruction of wildlife and the stupidity of Communist Party officials in the countryside. Many previously rejected works followed, including Vasily Grossman's saga of the Battle of Stalingrad, *Life and Fate*, and Anatoli Rybakov's *Children of the Arbat*, a novelistic indictment of the Stalin era.

By 1989 the cultural thaw had turned into a spring flood. More than 200 experimental theatre studios were active in Moscow alone. Artistic exiles and émigrés were welcomed home. Kazimir Malevich was reinstated as the "founding father" of Soviet modern art. New recognition was accorded the long-suppressed plays and prose works of Mikhail Bulgakov. Rock bands, no longer restricted by the censorship board, directors focused gained mass appeal.

Above all, the film industry exploded into vigorous life. Freed from the shackles of Goskino, the state film censorship board, directors focused on social ills: class resentments, alcoholism, domestic brutality, stifling bureaucracy. For the first time, films had explicit sex scenes, and television shows became far less inhibited.

While the country's cultural life was greatly invigorated by a transfusion of the best of six decades of banned Soviet and émigré art, the competition also exposed the mediocrity of many established artists whose development had so long been restricted. Commented Sergei Zalygin, editor in chief of the Moscow literary monthly *Novy Mir*: "Like Tolstoy and Dostoevsky in the past century, our artists need to find a new style and a new way of thinking if they hope to create a psychological portrait of society today."

**Poet Bella Akhmadulina poses for husband Boris Messerer in his studio. A fellow poet once called her "a fatal show-off", an "angel from another world"**

with a "beautiful, bratty tilt" to her chin.

# A BLESSED COUPLE

Bella and Boris Messerer are among the Soviet élite, distinguished citizens rewarded for their achievements with a lifestyle that would be considered comfortable in any society. Boris is an artist and set designer. Bella—known to her millions of fans by her maiden name, Akhmadulina—is a translator and one of the country's most famous poets, who often gives large, well-attended public readings. Her poetry is lyrical, deeply feminine and apolitical *(below)*.

While more ordinary citizens may be living in cramped quarters, the Messerer family—Bella and Boris, Bella's two young daughters from her previous marriages and their pet poodle and Alsatian— enjoy well-furnished homes in city and country. They have a three-room dacha, or country cottage, in the village of Peredelkino just 30 kilometres from Moscow. Here, nestled among the trees, are other wooden dachas of writers and editors. The houses were built by the Writers' Union for its most illustrious members; they may be owned outright or rented for a nominal fee. In addition to their Peredelkino dacha, the Messerers have a flat with studio *(left)* in an old Moscow building, where Boris paints in bold, contemporary style.

## DON'T GIVE ME ALL OF YOUR TIME

*Don't give me all of your time,*
*don't question me so often.*
*With eyes so true and faithful*
*don't try and catch my hands.*

*Don't follow in the Spring*
*my steps through pools of rain.*
*I know that of our meeting*
*nothing will come again.*

*You think it's pride that makes*
*me turn my back on you?*
*It's grief, not pride that holds*
*my head so very straight.*

Bella Akhmadulina, 1962

Standing tall in high heels, Bella recites her poems in an elaborately decorated Moscow concert hall. In the Soviet Union, such readings are second in popularity only to soccer; the poet Andrei Voznesensky once filled an ice-hockey stadium with more than 10,000 of his admirers.

Bella is interviewed by a Moscow television crew. Her face is well-known throughout the country, not only because of her poetry, but because of her frequent television appearances. She also once starred in a popular film, playing the part of a brash reporter.

Boris, who divides his time between his painting and set designs for theatre, opera and ballet productions, adjusts the model of a modern stage set he is working on. Boris is also an accomplished printmaker and keeps a large hand-press in his studio.

After writing poetry all morning long, Bella begins preparations for lunch in her modern, well-equipped Moscow kitchen. Hanging on the wall behind her are dough sculptures.

At day's end Bella and Boris relax in front of a fire while she reads him some of her fan mail. Fireplaces are rare in Moscow, where most housing is built from prefabricated sections.

# AT HOME IN CITY AND COUNTRY

Boris wears modish ski clothes—including a woollen cap from Lake Placid, New York, scene of the 1980 Winter Olympics—as he wields a wooden shovel to clear snow from the steps of the couple's country house.

Entertaining a guest in their pine-panelled dacha, Bella lays a table with a variety of cold appetizers—as well as imported Danish beer with which to wash down the food. On the far left is Bella's younger daughter, Lisa.

Holding an AK-47 rifle, a schoolgirl
stands guard at a World War II
monument in Irkutsk, Siberia. The
majority of Soviet children belong to
the Young Pioneers—described in
their charter as "convinced fighters
for the Communist party cause".

# THE OMNIPOTENT STATE

On February 19, 1990, two Soviet cosmonauts returned to earth from the orbital space station *Mir*. They had been absent for 166 days. In that brief span, however, the world had changed so radically that they could have been forgiven for imagining that their space journey had projected them decades ahead in time.

When their *Soyuz TM-9* blasted off in the previous September, East and West were firmly set apart—demarcated by the Berlin Wall, by fortifications dividing two Germanies, and by the Communist buffer nations of Bulgaria, Czechoslovakia, Hungary, Poland and Romania. Now the cosmonauts found the Berlin Wall a mere quarry for souvenir hunters. After nearly 45 years of division, German reunification was suddenly recognized as inevitable, and the vast East European Soviet bloc was disintegrating as all the buffer states began to throw off the yoke of one-party Communist rule.

Moreover, through massive reductions in nuclear and conventional armaments, and by the gradual withdrawal of all Russian troops in East European countries, the Soviet Union was easing the military tension between East and West. As a result, in March 1990, the hands of the "Doomsday Clock"—a symbol devised in 1947 by leading atomic scientists to dramatize the risk of nuclear war—were moved back four minutes, to 10 minutes to midnight.

Meanwhile, the Soviet Union had experienced the greatest civil unrest since the forging of the multinational empire in the 1920s. Ethnic violence had exploded in many regions, most notably in Armenia and Azerbaijan. To varying degrees, the republics of Estonia, Latvia, Lithuania, Georgia and Moldavia had witnessed an upsurge of public protest in pursuit of independence. And, in January 1990, President Gorbachev had announced that a law was being drafted to allow individual republics to secede from the Soviet Union.

But perhaps the most astounding event of all had occurred just 12 days before the cosmonauts returned to earth. On February 7, the Central Committee of the Soviet Union Communist Party had agreed to break with more than 70 years of tradition and surrender the party's exclusive right to rule—a decision widely interpreted as signalling the beginning of the end of the world's largest and most powerful totalitarian system.

Prodded by Gorbachev's three new instruments of *perestroika*, *glasnost* and *demokratizatsiya*, the Soviets had now tentatively begun to jettison many of their Communist principles in favour of the tenets that are at the heart of democratic capitalism: contested elections, pluralism, codified individual rights, private land ownership, market incentives and the reward of private enterprise. What amounted to a second Russian revolution had begun. It was hailed as perhaps the most momentous event of the second half of the 20th century.

With some justification, it was attributed largely to the vision, courage and persuasiveness of one man: Mikhail Gorbachev, a leader who was determined to rescue his people from their backwater and propel them into the modern industrial world. But the metamorphosis of the world's last empire was less a revolution than a somewhat haphazard process of accelerated evolution. Gorbachev had much in common with U.S. President Franklin D. Roosevelt who, faced with the Great Depression of the 1930s, declared: "The country needs bold, persistent experimentation. Take a method and try it; if it fails, admit it and try another. But above all, try something."

All the tries made by the Soviet Union and Eastern Europe from the late 1980s onwards had one common source: the need to rescue the U.S.S.R. from some 20 years of economic stagnation. One change led to the next as President Gorbachev began tinkering with an economic system constructed rather like a Russian doll, so that whenever he tackled one layer of problems he discovered another, more challenging, layer beneath. Ultimately he found that the structure was rotten to the core; that nothing less than a fundamental reshaping of the Soviet system, both political and economic, could bring his country stumbling and blinking in amazement into the light of a new and more prosperous era.

To appreciate how and why Gorbachev came to this radical conclusion, it is necessary to understand the state of the nation at the time of his election to supreme office, the

# 6

strengths and weaknesses of its political and economic structures, and the curious chain of events that preceded his appointment—at 54, the youngest man ever to become head of the Soviet Communist Party.

The state, according to Karl Marx, is an instrument of oppression. Marx envisaged a society in which workers and peasants would manage their own factories and land, and the state would "wither away". More than half a century after Marx's followers won control of the Russian Empire, that vision had still not been realized.

Supported by an immense military machine and an omnipresent internal security apparatus, the Kremlin sought to control every aspect of life. Inevitably, the state's reach exceeded its grasp. Underground factories and black markets made up a *nalevo*—"on the left"—economy challenging the official one. Dissident publications and bold demonstrations sporadically opposed official policies.

Nevertheless, in the mid-1980s, the state was still the heart, if not the soul, of the Soviet Union, and the power behind the state was the Communist Party. At every level, the party made or affected all policy decisions. Party members numbered about 18 million, almost 10 per cent of the adult population, recruited from all segments of Soviet society. And all members belonged to one of about 400,000 primary party organizations based at their workplaces.

From there the party formed a colossal pyramid through city, district, regional and republic levels to the Central Committee, made up of about 500 members elected every five years to represent all parts of the U.S.S.R. At the apex was the Secretariat, serving as

After buying luxuries at a Moscow Beriozka Gastronom—one of a chain of stores accepting only foreign currency—a privileged state official enters his limousine. Its licence labels it a Central Committee car.

the party's general staff; and the Politburo, which met weekly to make the party's, and hence the nation's, policy decisions. One man, the party's General Secretary, chaired the Politburo and the Secretariat. He was first among equals, chief steward of power, *the* Soviet leader.

From the apex of power—whose pattern recurred in miniature at every level of Soviet society—the party ran the Soviet Empire. It exerted its will through government structures which, though organized like those in other countries, were always staffed in key positions by high party officials.

Ostensibly, the nation's parliament, the Supreme Soviet, was elected by the citizens of the U.S.S.R., as indeed were the subsidiary soviets at the republic and local levels. However, these elections were hardly free and open. Rather, they were examples of what the Russians wryly call *pokazukha*, meaning to make a show, to make things look different from reality. The process began a few months before the voting, with mass meetings held to nominate candidates.

Typically, these meetings were stage-

managed so that although three people were nominated for a single seat in the Supreme Soviet, only one of them—the one chosen by the party secretary of the district—could be elected. After a time, the dummy candidates graciously bowed out, leaving only the one candidate. This political gavotte was performed all over the country so that the nominations would produce a balanced, predetermined list of candidates: about a third of the 1,500 candidates would be important party functionaries, government ministers, and top military and police officers; the remainder provided token representation for various ethnic groups, occupations and even ages.

Although each candidate ran unopposed, an enormous election campaign was mounted. Everyone over 18 was eligible to cast a vote, and as much as 5 per cent of the electorate might be mobilized by the government to make sure that everyone did actually vote. These electioneers went door-to-door to campaign, to transport the voters to the polls—where refreshments were often served—and to carry ballot boxes to hospitals. The

voter then faced a ballot paper with one name on it. Dropping that ballot in the box constituted a "yes" vote. To cast a "no" ballot—writing in another name was forbidden—the voter had to strike out the name.

What counted for the Soviets was getting the voters to turn out, and official statistics invariably vindicated the effort as a success. After the 1982 local elections, *Pravda* reported that 99.98 per cent of the 177,995,382 eligible voters turned out. It was all *pokazukha*, of course. Elections remained a charade to demonstrate virtually unanimous support for the leadership and its policies.

Thus, the Communist Party was self-perpetuating, omnipotent and omnipresent. At its head, the General Secretary was the most powerful individual in the Soviet Union. But he, too, was locked into the political system, and he challenged it at his peril. Nikita Khrushchev, for example, held the post for 11 years, but he also made powerful enemies inside the party, with a vigorous campaign of de-Stalinization and reorganization of the party structure. Many upper-level *apparatchik*s saw their careers threatened and turned against him, finally ousting him from power at a meeting of the Central Committee in 1964.

Herein lay perhaps the greatest obstacle to changes in the system: those who advanced successfully up the party ladder joined a privileged class of perhaps a million people, including prominent writers, scientists, artists, athletes, military officers and government officials. They became the movers and shakers in Soviet society and, like leaders everywhere, expected large salaries and special privileges. For many of these *nachalniki*—

bosses—the most prized perquisite was foreign travel. At home they had access to spacious city apartments as well as country dachas, to private cars or even limousines, and to a network of exclusive hospitals and clinics. They could shop at special stores selling rare imported and domestic items—French cognac or just fresh fruit—as well as ordinary groceries at low prices. These perquisites were bestowed according to rank. A former bureaucrat recalls that even in the snack bars of the Kremlin, "there is a hierarchy: the higher the floor, the lower the prices and the wider and more luxurious the range of merchandise". American cigarettes and Scotch whisky, for example, were for the top floors only.

Though the perquisites of power could not be directly bequeathed to the next generation, the élite was self-perpetuating. Members were able to use their influence to arrange good education and important jobs for their sons and daughters.

The fact that privileges were accorded to the *nachalniki* was acknowledged, even though it contradicted the egalitarian ideal of Marxism: "From each according to his ability, to each according to his need." People were rewarded for their work, as in other social systems. Said Stalin in 1931: "Only people unacquainted with Marxism can have the primitive notion that the Russian Bolsheviks want to pool all the wealth and then share it out equally."

Thus, in the mid-1980s, as in the time of the tsars, society was still ruled from above by an autocratic élite. A Western politician likened the system to "one big corporation—U.S.S.R. Incorporated". The system, like a corporation, was responsible for everything

within its domain. Moreover, its most important business was indeed business. And in many respects it adhered to procedures typical of corporations. From a highly centralized bureaucracy in Moscow, the state ran the economy. With a few exceptions—collective farms, artisans' workshops, and some stores and services run as co-operatives—the nation's capital assets were state-owned and state-operated. Revenues from state enterprises, plus sales taxes on manufactured goods and a lower personal income tax, were the state's income; and its budget was always balanced.

The basic instrument through which the state controlled the economy was known as the Plan, with a capital P. It was really a complex of plans encompassing all state enterprises. It set production targets, fixed prices and allocated raw materials and labour. The Plan told a steel mill how many tonnes to produce, a restaurant how many meals to serve and a lawyer how many court cases to try.

The Plan emanated from the State Planning Commission—Gosplan—on the basis of priorities set by the Politburo, the major policy-making body of the Communist Party and in effect of the country. Once rubber-stamped by parliament, the Plan carried the force of law. "We live under a tyranny," a Soviet intellectual once remarked, "the tyranny of the Plan."

The various levels of the Plan covered periods ranging from a month to five years and were tailored to each enterprise. Westerners are most familiar with the national Five-Year Plans, which were promulgated to set goals for economic development.

Stalin launched the first Five-Year Plan in 1928. It gave top priority to the

# 6

development of heavy industry such as steelmaking, mining and the manufacture of machine tools. It and the following Plans, which had similar priorities, achieved spectacular successes. Their ruthless marshalling of the nation's enormous labour force and bountiful natural resources transformed a peasant-based economy into a modern industrial state.

The ability of this highly centralized economy to concentrate its resources

could be awesome. Consider, for example, the "hero project" that was the centrepiece for each Five-Year-Plan, serving as a showcase of Soviet industrial might to the world and a source of pride to the nation's own citizens.

During the early 1970s, the hero project was the construction of a mammoth lorry factory on the Kama River, about 965 kilometres east of Moscow. At a cost of over five billion dollars, Soviet engineers created the world's

largest self-contained manufacturing plant. Capable of producing 150,000 heavy vehicles a year virtually from scratch, the 60-square-kilometre complex was not merely an assembly plant: it had its own foundries and forges as well, and accommodation for 70,000 workers in a satellite city.

In the early 1980s, another hero project, the Baikal-Amur Mainline (BAM) was even more ambitious *(pages 58-65)*: a 3,200-kilometre-long railway through the remote and mountainous reaches of Eastern Siberia, strategically located several hundred kilometres north of the original Trans-Siberian Railway and linking up with Pacific ports.

True, Five-Year-Plans were achieved at appalling cost to the environment. Nevertheless, the fact remained that the peoples of the Soviet Union worked miracles in expanding industry and communications over such a vast and often forbidding land. By the

1980s, their nation ranked second only to the United States in overall industrial output and it was first in steelmaking, traditionally an index of basic economic power. Moreover, in spite of the low priority given by Plans to consumer goods, such production had increased enough to improve the quality of life in most regions.

At the same time, the Soviet Union had made extraordinary progress in scientific and technological research. By the mid-1980s, the Soviet scientific establishment was without equal in size. One and a half million researchers with advanced science degrees—one fourth of all such specialists in the world—were organized in a nationwide network of 3,000 institutes and in thousands of experimental laboratories and field stations.

At least half of this network came under the direct jurisdiction of Moscow's Academy of Sciences, which also operated a special Siberian station at Akademgorodok, or Academic City, a suburb of Novosibirsk in central Siberia, housing more than 40 individual research institutes and staffed by 3,000 scientists. Like other scientific workers in the U.S.S.R., they were granted high salaries and opportunities for travel abroad, as well as the great benefit of housing that, by Soviet standards, was luxurious.

By rewarding scientists with perquisites and prestige, the Soviet Union attracted a high proportion of its ablest youth into the scientific establishment. And by focusing their efforts, that establishment achieved huge successes. Beginning in 1957, Soviet specialists launched a series of space explorations that stunned the world: *Sputnik 1*, the first artificial satellite, which launched the space

**Despite sporadic campaigns to punish laziness, many Soviet workers, like this napping maintenance man, are idle on the job. Foreign observers and even the Soviets blame such indolence for the ills of the nation's economy.**

# AT WORK, FAMILY-STYLE

**Workers at the Leninsky plant remain in the factory orbit both on and off the job, cosseted by the services their workplace provides.**

In the year 1903, an official inspecting a Russian sugar factory was dismayed to find the workers living in huge, barracks-like dormitories. Thinking to improve their lot by providing them with a modicum of privacy, he proposed that partitions be erected between their beds—only to be met with a storm of objections from the workers. "Are we cattle, that we should be cooped up in stalls?" they protested.

This favouring of proximity over privacy survives undiminished among the workers of the 1980s— and Soviet authorities make the most of it. People who work together—party officials, military officers, newspaper editors, farm hands or factory machinists— are made to feel that they are members of a family, responsible for one another, dependent on one another and secure in their shared lives. Some workplaces provide employees with everything they need for their daily lives: residences, child-care centres, medical services, theatres and holiday accommodation. Not all workplaces offer services of equal quality, but the services are always better than those available in the outer world. They go with the job and end when the job ends. It is security not from cradle to grave, but from cradle to workbench.

This collective living can be seen at its idealized best at the Leninsky Komsomol Automobile Plant in Moscow *(above)*, known as AZLK from its Russian initials. A showplace displaying Soviet-style industry as it is meant to be seen, the plant is the second largest manufacturer of passenger vehicles in the country, producing 200,000 Moskvich compact cars a year. AZLK provides its several thousand workers with necessities, comforts and amusements, including apartment houses a bus ride away from the plant *(page 142)*, nurseries, clinics and a "Palace of Culture" that serves up entertainment to fill leisure hours.

Near a cluster of factory-sponsored blocks of flats, workers wait for a bus.

Children of Leninsky plant employees play in a toy-filled day-care centre.

Injured workers receive physiotherapy at a factory out-patient clinic.

For a nominal fee that is scaled to their wages, AZLK's working parents can place their children in one of 16 nurseries and kindergartens. Children are eligible for care in a nursery when they are only three months old; about 25 per cent of Soviet infants under the age of two spend eight to 12 hours a day in collective nurseries. However, some mothers and even some Soviet child psychologists object to such early separation of mother and baby; most Soviet women take advantage of the liberal maternity leave—a year off, including four months at full pay—to stay at home and take care of their infants themselves.

The daily regimen at a childcare centre at AZLK—or anywhere else—is determined in Moscow and transmitted by handbook to teachers throughout the land. The authorities do not stint on facilities. One Western correspondent noted that even in farm collectives, which are less sophisticated than AZLK, "the nursery was the brightest and certainly the cleanest spot on the premises, an obligatory stop on the official tour of the farm because the powers-that-be were so proud of it."

Children generally get top priority for fresh food and vitamins, as well as medical supervision. Health care for their elders is also provided by the workplace. Prestigious institutions such as the Academy of Sciences and the Bolshoi Ballet have special hospitals to serve their own members. Elsewhere, medical care is likely to be more routine. Workers may be lined up, hundreds at a time, for physical check-ups; the check-up procedure consists of the doctor walking down the line, asking each person in turn for complaints.

The AZLK factory provides more than an army-style sick call. It maintains eight medical stations in those of its shops where accidents are likely, as well as an out-patient clinic that provides continuing therapy for injured workers. A patient who needs any

**At an unusually well-stocked supermarket located near the factory gate, a young couple selects tea from a bin.**

medicines can obtain them at a factory dispensary.

The factory also lends a helping hand with food to ensure that the employed eat well, even if others do not. Most staples are usually available, most of the time, in state stores, but more desirable fare may be hard to find. If the markets run short of such Russian favourites as sausages, cheese and canned fish, the factories are often able to get special consignments. When

they do, the factory foremen quickly pass the word around that the foods are available and the workers can line up to buy their allocations to take home.

The enveloping, protective arm of the workplace is perhaps most conspicuous in the arrangements for activities to fill leisure hours. Sports, crafts and the performing arts are accessible to Soviet citizens practically everywhere, together with free instruction in

practical arts and crafts activities.

Such activites are well attended. The AZLK Palace of Culture, on the factory premises, includes a cinema, a 1,200-seat auditorium for staging amateur theatrical productions, a lending library, no less than 24 classes for folk dancing alone, and still others for gymnastics and ballet. In that, it is not unique; factories in Minsk, Togliatti, Gorky and perhaps half a dozen other cities in the Soviet

Backs to a notice board announcing shows and classes, three factory employees comment on a painting.

Workers swim in a 50-metre pool at a sports complex that also houses a skating rink, a gym and a stadium.

**Two workers display their acting skills onstage at the Palace of Culture, where amateur theatre productions go on year-round.**

Union have facilities as extensive, and even small work organizations will make some provision for cultural activities.

Such palaces of culture also arrange, through the unions, for holiday accommodation that ranges from simple camping tents up in the mountains to hotel rooms along the Baltic coast. When workers take time off, they take it together their fellows.

The ubiquity of their fellow workers gives the Russians what they describe as "elbow feeling", by which they mean a sense of their friends being at their elbows, ever ready with support—in other words, security.

Ironically, the one group of citizens for whom no one brings news of special sausage or fruit consignments are those who are most apt to miss food delicacies: the elderly. When Soviet citizens leave the work force, they go with pensions—but for elbow feeling they must look to their kin. Collective welfare is for those who produce in the workplace.

age, was followed in 1959 by the first unmanned probe to the moon and in 1961 by the first manned orbital flight. In the 1950s, Nobel prize-winning Soviet physicists Andrei Sakharov and Igor Tamm developed a theoretical basis for a device—the Tokomak—that promised safe, waste-free power from nuclear fission; 10 years later another team of Soviet physicists built the first of these machines. At about the same time, yet another team pioneered laser technology.

On a more immediately practical level, however, this record was very mixed. Soviet science and engineering had turned out many inventions later used in the West, including a surgical stapling gun, a pneumatic underground punch called a "hole hog" and a technique for turning coal into coal gas underground. Yet in many fields their technology still lagged far behind. In mathematics, for example, Soviet theoreticians ranked among the best in the world, but Soviet society remained at least a decade behind the West in development and application of computers. In most Soviet offices and stores, calculations were still being done with the abacus. On average, the U.S.S.R. imported 14 times as much machinery and equipment from the West as it exported to the West.

Such failings affected civilian technology more than the military. The bulk of investment in scientific research was being poured into its mammoth military effort. In the mid-1980s, probably 15 per cent or more of the Soviet gross national product (GNP, the value of all goods and services produced in a given year) was going to the military. In contrast the U.S. was spending about 6 per cent on defence.

The result of the huge expenditure

## SOVIET FIRSTS IN SPACE

**Soviet successes in space have been spectacular, as this list attests. But there have been failures, too. Several—costing four lives —marred development of the *Soyuz* craft *(above)*, designed for missions to space stations. Efforts to land men on the moon also apparently ended in frustration; Western observers believe three launches failed or were aborted.**

| | | |
|---|---|---|
| Oct 1957 | **SPUTNIK 1** | First artificial earth satellite launched |
| Nov 1957 | **SPUTNIK 2** | First satellite to collect biological data; carried dog Laika |
| Sep 1959 | **LUNA 2** | First lunar probe to hit the moon |
| Oct 1959 | **LUNA 3** | First photographs of far side of the moon |
| Apr 1961 | **VOSTOK 1** | First manned orbital flight (Cosmonaut Yuri Gagarin) |
| Jun 1963 | **VOSTOK 6** | First woman in space (Cosmonaut Valentina Tereshkova) |
| Oct 1964 | **VOSKHOD 1** | First three-man orbital flight |
| Mar 1965 | **VOSKHOD 2** | First space walk, lasting 20 minutes (Cosmonaut Alexei A. Leonov) |
| Jan 1966 | **LUNA 9** | First soft landing of a probe on the moon |
| Oct 1967 | **KOSMOS 186 KOSMOS 188** | First automatic rendezvous and docking of satellites |
| Jan 1969 | **SOYUZ 4 SOYUZ 5** | First link-up of two manned vehicles and transfer of crew |
| Oct 1969 | **SOYUZ 6** | First triple launch of manned ships |
| Nov 1970 | **LUNA 17** | First robot vehicle on the moon |
| Apr 1971 | **SALYUT 1** | First prototype of manned space station launched |
| Jul 1975 | **APOLLO/SOYUZ JOINT PROJECT** | First international rendezvous and docking in space by U.S. and Soviet crews; aimed at developing a space rescue capability |
| Jan 1978 | **SOYUZ 27** | First triple docking in space |
| Oct 1981 | **SOYUZ 35** | Record of 6 months living in space |
| Dec 1988 | **MIR** | Record of one year living in space |

was weaponry in staggering quantities. Moreover, the quality was relatively high—much higher than that of civilian products. A former worker in an armaments plant described the system: "Military officers sit in each factory—in the big factories, these are generals—and they operate with strict discipline. They are empowered to reject *brak* (substandard items), and they reject great quantities." If the *brak* had any potential civilian application— reject blankets, electrical switches, petrol engines—much of it was then dumped on the consumer market.

Some factories, making a single item, were subdivided into three sections: military, export and domestic civilian. They had separate work forces and assembly lines organized in a simple hierarchy: the military section had the most experienced and best-paid workers, the newest machinery, the most generous production schedules and the strictest quality control. The export section received second best, and the civilian section was stuck with what remained. As one Western journalist summed it up: "The Soviet Union has been first in space, first in tanks and last in ladies' lingerie."

The low priority accorded civilian goods was only one reason why they were often shoddy and in short supply. A more fundamental cause was the highly centralized, from-the-top-down command structure, which so often proved unwieldy and inefficient in terms of production and distribution. Soviet factory managers resorted to numerous stratagems in order to beat the imposed system. For example, a manager might understate actual production capacity, making certain his plant did not exceed the current quota by more than 1 or 2 per cent.

Otherwise his targets would be raised. (Workers, too, needed to take care not to be too productive or their individual piecework quotas could go up.)

At the same time, the manager would often accumulate hidden reserves of raw materials and labour to fulfil the Plan despite equipment breakdowns, absenteeism and supply shortages. "If you want a two-hump camel," a Russian saying goes, "you must order a three-hump camel. The system will shave off the extra hump." Under this top-heavy administrative system, whole van-loads of materials were liable to arrive late or simply never show up. A Soviet newspaper once reported that only 70 per cent of the trees harvested ever reached timber or pulp mills; the rest were presumably ruined or stolen—or never harvested in the first place. By the 1980s, stealing from the state was so common that it became the source of many Russian jokes.

Shortages were a particular problem in the Soviet economy because the system was so rigidly interlocked. A producer who was unable to secure a needed commodity from a supplier assigned to him by the central Plan could not then turn to another supplier. Many enterprises sought self-sufficiency, producing their own manufacturing machinery. Two thirds of the national stock of machine tools was dispersed among factories to make the machinery needed to manufacture their principal products. This dispersion helped to eliminate some supply bottlenecks, but it broke up what otherwise might have been a concentrated, specialized machinery-producing industry, and thus it added to the overall production inefficiency.

More ingenious managers followed the example of their Western counterparts: they made deals—but on a grand scale. In a true-to-life novel called *In Plain Russian*, by Vladimir Voinovich, the hero, a construction supervisor, desperately needs linseed oil to thin paint that is to be used in a new block of flats. After fruitless appeals to the official supply chief, he tries to secure the oil through a complicated series of swaps with his fellow supervisors. He has to draw up a detailed list of supplies each one needs, and supplies each has to spare. "A complete strategic plan," he laments, "and all for one barrel of linseed oil."

In spite of such inventiveness, bottlenecks persisted in the 1980s, and they set a wildly erratic monthly rhythm of production. In practically every kind of industrial plant, the pace of the month's work tended to move in three distinct 10-day periods, described by one Soviet worker as *spyachka*, or "hibernation"; *goryachka*, or "hot time"; and *likhoradka*, or "storming".

For the first 10 days of *spyachka*, key supplies were usually missing, many workers were absent, and little work was done. During the *goryachka* middle 10 days, parts started dribbling in from the suppliers and the pace picked up. In the final 10 days, the rest of the supplies arrived, and the manager, his bonuses dependent on meeting the monthly quota, threw in reserves of workers and put them all on overtime.

A typical factory turned out 80 per cent of its monthly quota in those 10 days of storming. Goods were tagged with the date of production, and consumers tried to shun anything made after the 20th of the month.

If storming and stratagems failed, the manager had one last resort for fulfilling the Plan: he falsified his report. A poultry breeder from Central Asia told how his state farm met the daily target of 100,000 eggs—by writing off "30,000 to 40,000 eggs as if they had been broken and fed to the chickens, even though those eggs never existed".

Not surprisingly, the inability of the official economy to meet consumer demands created a second, largely unofficial, economy to fill the gap. Operated by private entrepreneurs, this parallel economy was part legal, part illegal; and even the illegal part was winked at if it was on a small scale.

Some professionals who worked for the state, such as physicians, were permitted to moonlight at home. Workers on state and collective farms were allowed to cultivate private gardens and sell their produce for whatever the market would bear. With these exceptions, however, private enterprise remained outside the law in the Soviet Union, and most of the second economy operated underground.

At its everyday level, this *nalevo* economy consisted of exchanges of favours and services, moonlighting by plumbers and other craftworkers, and the private selling of scarce goods such as cars *(page 21)*. Nevertheless, *nalevo* manufacturing and retail sales became big business, amounting to 10 per cent or more of the gross national product.

The mainstays of the underground economy were the *fartsovshchiki*—the black-market merchants who set up shops in cafés, on street corners or even in public toilets. The magazine *Literaturnaya gazeta*, investigating the black market, once sent a reporter to the city of Krasnodar near the Black Sea with instructions to buy a toothbrush, soap, razor blades, shaving cream, underclothes, socks and writing paper. The reporter spent a day scouring the government stores and could not find a single item. Then he turned to *fartsovshchiki* and quickly finished his shopping.

Some *fartsovshchiki* were officially acknowledged when the police felt compelled to act. A Lithuanian lawyer, Elizabeth Tyntareva, started small, peddling coveted articles such as sunglasses and women's wigs. Gradually she branched out into gold rings, watches, jeans and umbrellas, and developed a regular clientele among holidaymakers on the Baltic. By 1980, when she was arrested and sent to prison for 12 years, Tyntareva had four assistants and a mail-order service.

In the early 1980s, as the black market continued to expand, many underground goods were smuggled in from the West or bought from foreigners who obtained them in *beriozki*—special government stores reserved for foreign tourists and diplomats. But surprising quantities of illicit goods, ranging from sweaters to recordings of Western popular music, were made within the Soviet Union itself by the underground industries.

In these remarkable establishments, clandestine entrepreneurs literally used the machinery of the state to undercut the official economy. They operated under the same roofs and same names as the state-owned factories. And while the state factory produced under the government Plan, the factory-within-a-factory was running a second shift—with the same workers and same equipment—to make illicit goods in secret. The underground entrepreneur got the supplies, paid the workers and reaped the profits—but used capital investment unwittingly furnished by the state. And there was a share for the officials who earnt it by looking the other way.

At the same time, underground entrepreneurs had to avoid conspicuous consumption so as not to attract attention. Some found legal sources of income to explain their relatively high spending. A big winner in the government lottery might be paid two or three times his winnings to turn over his lucky ticket to the *nalevo* magnate, who could use it to justify his high income. Others of the underground rich converted their roubles into dollars, precious stones and gold, and hid such valuables, hoarding wealth that might never be spent.

For many, unable to use much of their *nalevo* income on anything else, the main indulgence was gambling. At any of the several secret salons in major cities, they could show their wealth freely,—enjoy good food and drink, play cards and roulette, and, for an evening at least, feel the euphoria of spending recklessly money they had risked so much to accumulate.

In economic matters, however, only extreme cases provoked the government to exercise its right to regulate all facets of life. In other matters it was much less tolerant. In the early 1980s, political views remained subject to stringent control, and deviations from the party line put the dissenter at grave risk. Although the Soviet Constitution guaranteed freedom of expression and many other rights, it also forbade their exercise if deemed detrimental to "the interest of society or the state", and it flatly banned all anti-Soviet agitation.

To watch over political behaviour, the state maintained a ministerial-level police agency, the Committee for State Security—better known by its initials

# DÉTENTE ON THE HIGH SEAS

Putting aside political differences, the Union of Soviet Socialist Republics and the United States joined forces in 1976 in a surprising venture: they founded a profit-making business called Marine Resources. Today 21 Soviet ships like the one on the left regularly enter the offshore waters of the United States and take on board fish that have been caught for them by American fishermen.

The company is owned fifty-fifty by the Bellingham Cold Storage company of Washington, and the Soviet Ministry of Fisheries. Every autumn, representatives of the two countries meet in Moscow, and there they go over figures projecting the availability of fish and the size of the next season's market. Then, sometime in late January or early February, Soviet ships leave Siberian ports and rendezvous with American trawlers in the Bering Sea, in the Gulf of Alaska or off the Washington-Oregon coast. American observers live aboard the ships to monitor the size of the catch and to see that Soviet crews do not fish on their own while they are in American waters.

The ships are floating factories, equipped to sort, clean, and salt or freeze the catch that they receive from the American trawlers. Some of the larger factory ships— which can process more than 300 tonnes of fish a day—also double as service vessels, providing smaller ones with fuel, water and supplies. Fish deemed unfit for human consumption are reduced to fish meal for use as animal feed or fertilizer.

Once their lockers are full, the factory ships either transfer their cargo to other vessels for transport back to the U.S.S.R. or, at the season's end, deliver it there themselves. From the Siberian port of Nakhodka, Marine Resources distributes fish throughout the Soviet Union and to 16 other countries in Europe and Asia.

A Soviet ship hauls in fish caught for her by American fishermen in U.S. waters.

Pollock and hake crowd the deck before being hoisted into the hold for processing.

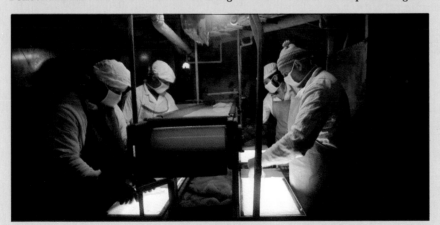

Below deck, surgically masked processors examine fish, checking for parasites.

# 6

in Russian, KGB. The KGB employed some 700,000 agents for domestic surveillance; one of every 250 adult Soviet citizens could thus be a KGB operative. Many of them were sent to the personnel departments of factories, government agencies and universities.

Full-time agents were supplemented by tens of thousands of casual workers paid by the KGB as informers and known contemptuously by most Russians as *stukachi*, or squealers. In Moscow apartment buildings, for example, residents would automatically presume that the little old lady who operated the lift was a KGB informer, paid to report on suspicious events such as a visit by a foreigner.

Anyone arrested for suspected subversion faced a justice system heavily weighted towards the interest of the state. Consider, for example, the case of Nikolai, a small-town factory worker who was arrested for painting angry complaints on the factory wall: "Why is our pay so low?" "Why is there no meat in the stores?"

Nikolai was charged with "political hooliganism". The pre-trial investigation was handled by the procurator—a state prosecutor with powers much broader than those of his Western counterparts. The procurator established guilt or innocence before any trial was held. The purpose of the trial was to decide punishment.

Nikolai appeared before a People's Court, a judge and two people's assessors—rubber-stamp lay jurists chosen, like the judge, without opposition in local elections. Testimony followed a line agreed upon by Nikolai's defence lawyer and the procurator: Nikolai was a drunkard who did not know what he was doing when he painted the graffiti. His lawyer hoped

this line would mitigate the severity of the sentence. Nikolai got seven years' exile in a far corner of Siberia.

In Stalin's time, it would have been much worse. Citizens accused of political offences were tortured into confessions, tried secretly by police tribunals and either executed or shipped off to a living death in the infamous Gulag— the Soviet Union's vast network of labour camps.

Nevertheless, in the early 1980s, over a quarter of a century after his death, all the basic apparatus of Stalin's Soviet Union remained intact. It was still an arch-authoritarian, single-party empire; a military, industrial and bureaucratic monolith, with state control of all means of production. Moreover, the Kremlin was still dominated by former Stalin protégés. Andrei Gromyko, for example, was in his third decade as Foreign Minister. Another septuagenarian, Leonid Brezhnev, had been in supreme power for 18 years—only the fourth leader of the Soviet Union since the 1917 Revolution.

In November, 1982, when President Brezhnev died, the need for social and economic reform was already glaring. The 1970s had seen living standards rise dramatically, to the point where the Soviet Union was almost a full-blooded consumer society. But since then, there had been a steady economic decline, with falling industrial growth, a succession of agricultural disasters, and ever-increasing corruption and inefficiency. It became clear that the material progress of the past decade had been a blip rather than a trend, the consequence of a switch in investment priorities from heavy industry to consumer production coinciding with the commissioning of numerous factories built in the 1960s.

But even new Soviet factories lagged at least a generation behind their Western counterparts in efficiency and quality. The typical Soviet plant's labour productivity was a paltry one third of the average level of factories in non-Communist countries. At the same time, Soviet plants used two to three times as much energy and raw material as Western factories consumed for the same amount of output. Restricted by the overcentralized command economy, the factories proved to be incapable of meeting the rising demand for consumer goods.

During President Brezhnev's regime, many economic experts had tentatively put forward new ideas to encourage initiative and enterprise. But any hopes of radical change now vanished as the elderly hierarchy entrenched itself by electing another traditionalist to supreme power: 68-year-old Yuri Andropov, a former chief of the KGB. Fifteen months later, Andropov died from kidney disease. Again the old guard secured its privileged position by electing his successor, Konstantin Chernenko, a white-haired Siberian who had been a close associate of Brezhnev and who was known to suffer from emphysema.

At 72, Chernenko was the oldest man to take over the Soviet leadership. His tenure—just 13 months—was to be the shortest in Kremlin history. Thus, the Soviet Union had lost three leaders in as many years; and all the while its economic crisis had been allowed to deepen through postponement of any radical reforms.

It was following these freak circumstances, when the pressing need for continuity in leadership could no longer be ignored, that 54-year-old Mikhail Gorbachev came to power. At last the Soviet Union had a General Secretary who was modern in outlook and sufficiently young to lead the country into the 21st century. But the challenge he faced was an awesome one. Change had been resisted at all levels for so long that it now seemed improbable that the Soviet Union's outdated totalitarian system could be reformed without the risk of provoking a political cataclysm.

The achievements of Mikhail Gorbachev as a fledgling statesman are now legendary. In his first five years as Soviet leader he had such an extraordinary impact on international politics that the age-old Cold War between East and West was suddenly judged to be ended, and U.S. President George Bush publicly announced, "We welcome the Soviet Union back into the world order". At the end of the 1980s, the Western press popularly named him "the man of the decade". Some even nominated him "the man of the century".

Gorbachev's fresh approach to foreign affairs was signalled from the moment he took supreme office. On March 11, 1985, in his first official pronouncement, he praised détente with the West and called for a reduction in arms stockpiles. The following month he announced a 10-month freeze in the deployment of medium-range missiles aimed at Western Europe. Thereafter, step by step, he initiated spectacular progress towards the first-ever deep cuts in nuclear weapons.

When Gorbachev came to power, the United States was proposing a one third cut in strategic nuclear weapons, the Soviet Union only a 25 per cent reduction. At the 1985 Geneva summit, Gorbachev raised the stakes by calling for a 50 per cent cut. In 1987, at the Washington summit, he and U.S. President Reagan signed the first treaty to reduce their nuclear arsenals.

The following year, in a momentous speech to the U.N. General Assembly, Gorbachev outlined his vision of a Europe no longer divided into military blocs and called for a "new world order" in international relations. He had already ordered the withdrawal of all Soviet troops from Afghanistan. Now he announced unilateral military cuts on an unprecedented scale. In under two years, the Soviet armed forces would be cut by half a million, a 10 per cent reduction in manpower; also, 800 combat aircraft and a quarter of all Soviet tanks and artillery in Europe were to be scrapped.

It was not, of course, an entirely altruistic gesture. The cuts would bring a twofold boost to the stagnant Soviet economy. It would be relieved of some 14 per cent of the country's enormous military budget—the heaviest of all burdens on the U.S.S.R. At the same time, Gorbachev hoped that improved international relations would boost trade. He and his advisers had concluded that the Soviet Union could no longer pursue national prosperity in isolation. Thus, he told the United Nations: "The world economy is becoming a single organism and no state, whatever its social system or economic status, can normally develop outside it." Four months later, in London, he stated quite bluntly: "Our economic reform presupposes the Soviet Union's closer integration into the world economy."

It was logical that his economic reforms should next focus on the East European buffer states—countries that had failed dismally to prosper under Communist rule. For more than four decades, the Soviet Union's links with these countries had proved counterproductive. In 1989 Gorbachev attributed their economic failures to "miscalculations by the ruling parties" and he announced that the Soviet Union was no longer willing to prop up their economies with charitable supplies of oil and raw materials. In future, they would have to find their own solutions and eventually become entirely self-supporting.

All at once, the Communist regimes of Eastern Europe were no longer firmly bound to Moscow and, deprived of their ecomomic crutches, they rapidly bowed to internal pressure for liberalizing reforms. In August, Poland became the first country in the Soviet bloc to appoint a non-Communist leader. That same month, Hungary opened its border with Austria to allow East Germans to flee to the West, and soon afterwards its Communist leaders voted to become social democrats. Meanwhile, on a visit to East Berlin, Gorbachev emphasized the need for fundamental reforms in East Germany and warned that countries were in danger if they failed to react to the "impulses" of the times. The East Germans reacted almost at once, beginning with the ousting from power of their hard-line Communist leader, Erich Honecker.

At home, the impact of Gorbachev's unorthodox leadership was no less extraordinary. Within five years, by way of his highly volatile mixture of *glasnost* and *perestroika*, he changed the social and political life of the Soviet Union. Again, economic considerations were the key to his actions. Having initially introduced moderate reforms without success, Gorbachev and his advisers concluded that major

# 6

economic growth could only be achieved by radical changes in the social order—changes that involved removing all traces of the Stalinist tyranny that had stifled initiative and creativity for so long. A quarter of a century before, Nikita Khrushchev had attempted to de-Stalinize the Soviet system. But he had tackled the problem from the top, and in seeking to reform the privileged, he had been eventually overthrown by them.

Gorbachev, in contrast, deliberately chose to stimulate political reform by encouraging pressure from below.

With the advent of *glasnost* in 1987, people were no longer liable to arrest under Article 70 of the constitution for "anti-Soviet propaganda and agitation". The floodgates were now open to a torrent of free expression—in the press, on television, and in the streets. Subsequently, with the introduction of

Sergei Batovrin, the leader of a pacifist group, stares from the window of a psychiatric hospital where he was held for a month. Until 1987, such confinement was the fate of many dissidents.

relatively free elections, popular revolts in the provinces resulted in the overthrow of numerous hard-line party leaders.

In this new climate of political unrest, Gorbachev had the support he needed to tackle the party bureaucracy head-on: to rid himself of arch-reactionaries in the Kremlin, to create new political institutions and, most remarkably, to pave the way for political pluralism by persuading the ruling Communist Party Central Committee to scrap Article 6 of the constitution which guaranteed the party's exclusive right to rule.

His flirtation with political freedom, however, was fraught with danger. For seven decades, the all-powerful Communist Party had been the cement that held together more than 100 nationalities within the heterogeneous Soviet Empire. Now this mortar was seriously weakened by exposure of past and present faults in the party system. The result was a massive upsurge in nationalism that Gorbachev found increasingly difficult to contain.

Large though the issues of nationalism loomed, Gorbachev's most pressing problem remained the economy. Five years after coming to power, he was nowhere near to extricating the country from the crisis that all along had spurred his sensational policies. Indeed, in terms of everyday living standards, the Soviet economy had decidedly worsened. Of course, the success or failure of *perestroika* was not to be judged by results over a mere five-year period. As the poet Bulat Okudzhava, a veteran advocate of reform, observed: "During the past 70 years, a new man has been created who is obedient and easily frightened. What has been created over decades

cannot be undone in a day." The fact remained, however, that Gorbachev's first stage of *perestroika* was fundamentally flawed because it weakened the old rigidly centralized command system without establishing an effective market system in its place.

It was in 1987 that Gorbachev took the first tentative step towards introducing a market system. He allowed individuals to form privately owned, profit-sharing co-operative enterprises to supplement and even compete with state-owned projects. The primary goal was to breed a new class of entrepreneurs and inject vitality into the laggard consumer goods and services industries. The new co-operatives would also pay taxes and, in theory at least, create new jobs for workers released by a much-needed pruning of the vast bureaucracy.

At first, the programme was limited mainly to high-visibility services such as taxis and cafés. By 1989, however, more than two million people were employed in a vast range of co-operatives and private businesses, from restaurants and translators to computer maintenance outfits and operators of privately owned pay toilets. *Izvestiya* reported: "The labour productivity of workers in co-operatives is three, five and even 10 times higher than in ordinary production."

In some areas, Gorbachev's brave new world of self-management was ushered in with conspicuous success. For example, the Lenin Factory near Michurinsk, some 350 kilometres south-west of Moscow, had gained notoriety in 1986 when criminal investigators broke up an organized crime ring trading in stolen merchandise. The factory, which makes auto parts, was subsequently "leased out" to

*kooperatischchiki.* By 1989, output had tripled, pilfering had plummeted, and the chief caretaker no longer found enough empty vodka bottles to necessitate a twice-daily trash-run into town.

The 130 co-operative members of the Lenin Factory were now earning on average about two and a half times the norm for factory workers, and at last production was meeting demand. Ironically, too, the changeover resulted in a greater sense of equality. Since the managers leased the factory, they had to account for every kopeck and could no longer afford a lifestyle far superior to that of the workers.

Other entrepreneurial ventures had mixed fortunes. Before *perestroika*, Andrei Fedorov had run a state-owned restaurant in Moscow, but in 1987 he started his own bistro, which within a year was making a handsome profit. Fedorov planned to improve his service by buying a farm, so ensuring a supply of quality produce and meat. But in seeking the requisite permits, he found himself continually blocked by bureaucratic red tape. He remarked, "Rather than create opportunities for real competition, these ministries are trying to tie our hands. They say what I want to do isn't necessary. They say we are not part of socialism."

Other entrepreneurs faced a variety of problems. Some became targets of organized crime, being forced to pay bribes or offer phoney jobs in return for "protection". Many were criticized for the high prices they charged— usually at least twice as high as in state shops—and accused of exploitation.

But the greatest difficulty lay in the system, which shackled free enterprise to the top-heavy bureaucracy of old. To operate, private businessmen required permission from the local authority, which provided both registration and premises. Many found themselves being harassed by reform-resistant bureaucrats. They suffered from high rents and arbitrary taxation, which pushed their prices higher. And the majority of factories were still under the thumb of Moscow planners; the industrial ministries, forced to fulfil their five-year plans, were all too slow in relinquishing their power.

That meant that private factories relied on Moscow for merchandise orders and financial support. Since most factories answered only to bureaucrats instead of consumers, finished merchandise was often shoddy or simply the wrong type of product to meet the demand. And since private factories generally depended on public ones for supplies, the government could fix the price of the private factories' raw materials and thus drastically limit their financial autonomy.

Another difficult aspect of restructuring was the need to close down unprofitable factories. Bankruptcies were now legal, but few occurred because bureaucrats were loath to reduce their domain and fearful of the unrest that would be caused by throwing employees out of work. Moscow ministries preferred instead to merge unsuccessful enterprises into stronger ones.

Meanwhile, *perestroika* had also failed to have a significant impact in another crucial direction: the encouragement of private agriculture. From the start, Gorbachev had promoted "contract" farming, whereby small groups of families could enter into an agreement to handle a certain portion of a collective farm's crops, land or livestock. In 1990 a new law, approved by the Supreme Soviet, went further: it gave people the right to lease land and bequeath its use to their children in perpetuity.

The new law was intended to improve the abysmal performance of the collective and state farms and so raise food production. Despite huge investment, the national shortage of food, especially fresh fruit, vegetables and dairy products, was the greatest source of popular discontent. The U.S.S.R. was spending more than 100 billion dollars, roughly 15 per cent of its budget, subsidizing food, and imported some 40 million tonnes of grain every year. But wastage was appalling: as much as a third of produce rotted before it reached consumers. One Soviet collective farmer, it was estimated, fed only seven to nine people; in contrast, a Dutch farmer provided food for at least 112.

Unfortunately, the move towards land-leasing, like the introduction of co-operatives, was half-hearted. The new legislation acknowledged ideological objections to private property ownership and the buying and selling of land. It only allowed plots to be leased at prices set by the local soviets to which their ownership had been delegated; and it left peasants with the lurking fear that the land they leased could be reclaimed at any time.

Under *perestroika*, Gorbachev had not been marching headlong towards capitalism but rather attempting to reinvent Marxism by creating socialist markets and socialist competition. Five years after his coming to office, private ownership of the means of production, whether land or factories, was still prohibited. Individuals could not hire workers with a view to profiting from their labour. There was a noncompetitive banking system, and no stock market for financing private ventures. Most damagingly, there was no

rational price system; with thousands of prices still set by state fiat rather than by supply and demand, the former never equalled the latter.

In 1990, Gorbachev's top economic adviser, Deputy Prime Minister Leonid Abalkin, acknowledged that "almost every sector of the economy is in a shambles". The budget deficit—caused in part by transfusion to anaemic factories and subsidies for food and housing—was an estimated 11 per cent of the GNP. The rouble, arbitrarily said to be worth 1.60 dollars but not freely convertible into dollars or

any other Western currency, brought as little as 10 cents on the black market. Paper incomes had risen but the standard of living had fallen sharply; and, in conditions akin to a wartime economy, shortages encouraged hoarding and panic buying.

Mr Abalkin's solutions to the dilemma were as radical as any plans of the Gorbachev era. He proposed to free all trade and commerce from state control, reform pricing policy and introduce a new social security system. A stock exchange and commercial banks would be established, state

monopolies privatized and the tax system revamped. "We can no longer continue balancing between two stools," pronounced the Deputy Prime Minister—predicting, however, that an economic revolution would be very difficult and painful.

That prediction was one of the few that could be made with confidence in the metamorphosing Soviet Empire. Another was made in 1990 by Sergei Zalygin, editor of the crusading literary monthly *Novy Mir.* "How it will end we do not know," he said, " but there is no turning back now."

# ACKNOWLEDGEMENTS

The index for this book was prepared by Susanne Atkin. For their help with this volume, the editors also wish to thank: Vasily Aksyonov, George Washington University, Washington, D.C.; Cyril E. Black, Princeton University, Center of International Studies, Princeton, New Jersey; James E. Cole, Economic Research Service, U.S. Department of Agriculture, Washington, D.C.; Frederick Crory, U.S. Army Cold Regions Research and Engineering Laboratory, Hanover, New Hampshire; Murray Feshbach, Kennedy Institute of Ethics, Georgetown University, Washington, D.C.; Steven A. Grant, U.S.I.C.A., Washington, D.C.; Dmitry Grigorieff, Georgetown University, Washington, D.C.; George W. Hoffman, Department of Geography, The University of Texas, Austin, Texas; Deborah A. Kaple, Wharton Econometric Forecasting Associates, Washington, D.C.; John W. Kiser, Kiser Research, Inc., Washington, D.C.; Gail Lapidus, Kennan Institute for Advanced Studies, Woodrow Wilson International Center for Scholars, Washington, D.C.; Sander H. Lee, Howard University, Washington, D.C.; Fairy von Lilienfeld, Institute of History and Theology of the Christian East, School of Theology, University of Erlangen/Nürnberg, West Germany; Nancy Lubin, Office of Technology Assessment, U.S. Congress, Washington, D.C.; Paul E. Lydolph, Department of Geography, University of Wisconsin, Milwaukee, Wisconsin; Dmitry Mikheyev, Arlington, Virginia; Henry Morton, Queens College, Flushing, New York; Victor Mote, University of Houston, Texas; Bruce W. Nelan, *Time*, Washington, D.C.; Rose Nelan, Fairfax, Virginia; David E. Powell, Russian Research Center, Harvard University, Cambridge, Massachusetts; Elisavietta Artanoff Ritchie, Washington, D.C.; Richard M. Robin, Slavic Department, George Washington University, Washington, D.C.; Vladimir G. Treml, Duke University, Durham, North Carolina; Adam B. Ulam, Director of Russian Research Center, Harvard University, Cambridge, Massachusetts; Jan Vánous, Wharton Econometric Forecasting Associates, Washington, D.C.

These sources were particularly useful in the preparation of this volume: "Russia's Underground Millionaires" by Konstantin Simis, *Fortune*, June 29, 1981; and *Inside Russian Medicine* by William A. Knaus, Everest House/ Dodd, Mead & Co., Inc., 1981. The editors are also indebted to the following quoted sources: *Involuntary Journey to Siberia* by Andrei Amalrik by permission of Harcourt Brace Jovanovich, Inc. Fyodor Dostoevsky: *The Devils* trans. David Magarshack (Penguin Classics, Revised edition 1971). Fyodor Dostoevsky: *Crime & Punishment* trans. David Magarshack (Penguin Classics 1966). "A Letter from Moscow" by Joseph Kraft in the *New Yorker*. *Russian Journal* by Andrea Lee by permission of Random House, Inc. *The Romanovs* by W. Bruce Lincoln. A Dial Press Book by permission of Doubleday & Co., Inc. *Peter the Great: His Life and His World* by Robert K. Massie by permission of Alfred A. Knopf, Inc. *Land of the Firebird: The Beauty of Old Russia* by Suzanne Massie by permission of Simon and Schuster, Inc. *Lectures on Russian Literature* by Vladimir Nabokov translated and reprinted by permission of Harcourt Brace Jovanovich, Inc. *U.S.S.R.: The Corrupt Society* by Konstantin Simis by permission of Simon and Schuster, Inc. *In Plain Russian* by Vladimir Voinovich by permission of Farrar, Straus and Giroux, Inc.

# PICTURE CREDITS

# BIBLIOGRAPHY

## BOOKS

Akhmatova, Anna, *Poems of Anna Akhmatova.* Atlantic Monthly Press, Little, Brown, 1973.

Amalrik, Andrei, *Involuntary Journey to Siberia.* Harcourt Brace Jovanovich, 1970.

Barrett, David B., *World Christian Encyclopaedia.* Oxford University Press, 1982.

Berlin, Isaiah, *Russian Thinkers.* Hogarth Press, 1978.

Berliner, Joseph, *Innovation Decision in Soviet Industry.* Massachusetts Institute of Technology Press, 1976.

Billington, James H., *The Icon and the Axe.* Vintage, 1970.

Brine, Jenny, Maureen Perrie and Andrew Sutton, eds., *Home, School and Leisure in the Soviet Union.* George Allen & Unwin, 1980.

Bronfenbrenner, Urie, *Two Worlds of Childhood, U.S. and U.S.S.R.* Russell Sage, 1970.

Brown, Archie, John Fennell, Michael Kaser and H. T. Willetts, eds., *The Cambridge Encyclopaedia of Russia and the Soviet Union.* Cambridge University Press, 1982.

Carrère d'Encausse, Helene, *Decline of an Empire.* Newsweek Books, 1980.

Center for International Studies, *Attitudes of Major Soviet Nationalities.* Massachusetts Institute of Technology Press, 1973.

Congressional Quarterly, *The Soviet Union.* Congressional Quarterly, Inc., 1982.

Connolly, Violet, *Siberia Today and Tomorrow.* Collins, 1975.

Conquest, Robert, ed., *Industrial Workers in the U.S.S.R.* Bodley Head, 1967.

Conquest, Robert, *V. I. Lenin.* Fontana, 1972.

Crankshaw, Edward, ed., *Khrushchev Remembers.* Little, Brown, 1970.

Dewdney, John C., *A Geography of the Soviet Union.* Pergamon, 1979.

Dmytryshyn, Basil, *U.S.S.R.: A Concise History.* Charles Scribner's Sons, 1978.

Dornberg, John, *The Soviet Union Today.* Dial Press, 1976.

Dostoevsky, Fyodor:
*Crime and Punishment.* Penguin, 1954.
*The Devils.* Penguin, 1957.

Dyck, H. W., *Boris Pasternak.* Twayne, 1972.

Ehre, Milton, ed., *The Theater of Nikolay Gogol.* Transl. by Früma Gottschalk. The University of Chicago Press, 1980.

Feshbach, Murray, *The Soviet Union: Population Trends and Dilemmas.* Population Reference Bureau, 1982.

Granick, David, *Red Executive.* Coser, Lewis & Powell, 1979.

Hecht, Leo, *The U.S.S.R. Today: Facts and Interpretations.* Scholasticus. 1982.

Hough, Jerry F., and Merle Fainsod, *How the Soviet Union is Governed.* Harvard University Press, 1979.

Jacoby, Susan, *Inside Soviet Schools.* Hill and Wang, 1974.

Joint Economic Committee, Congress of the United States, *Soviet Economy in a Time of Change.* Vols. I and II, Washington, D.C., 1979.

Kaiser, Robert G., *Russia, The People and the Power.* Pocket Books, 1976.

Kaiser, Robert G., and Hannah Jopling, *Russia From the Inside.* Hutchinson, 1980.

Keefe, Eugene K., et al., *Area Handbook for the Soviet Union.* U.S. Government Printing Office, 1971.

Knaus, William A., *Inside Russian Medicine.* Everest House, 1981.

Komarov, Boris, *The Destruction of Nature in the Soviet Union.* Transl. by Michel Vale and Joe Hollander. Sharpe, 1980.

Lapidus, Gail Warhofsky, *Women in Soviet Society.* University of California Press, 1978.

Lee, Andrea, *Russian Journal.* Faber & Faber, 1982.

Lincoln, W. Bruce, *The Romanovs.* Weidenfeld & Nicolson, 1982.

Lydolph, Paul E., *Geography of the U.S.S.R.,* Misty Valley Publishing, 1979.

Madariaga, Isabel De, *Russia in the Age of Catherine the Great.* Weidenfeld & Nicolson, 1981.

Mandelstam, Nadezhda, *Hope Against Hope.* Collins/Harvill Press, 1981.

Massie, Robert K., *Peter the Great, His Life and World.* Gollancz, 1981.

Massie, Suzanne, *Land of the Firebird.* Hamish Hamilton, 1981.

McDowell, Bart, *Journey Across Russia.* National Geographic, 1977.

Medish, Vadim, *The Soviet Union.* Prentice-Hall. 1981.

Mowat, Farley, *The Siberians.* Little, Brown, 1970.

Nabokov, Vladimir, *Lectures on Russian Literature.* Weidenfeld & Nicolson, 1982.

Peskov, Vasili, *This Is My Native Land.* Progress Publishers, 1976.

Pond, Elizabeth, *Russia Perceived.* Gollancz, 1981.

Reavey, George, ed., *The New Russian Poets, 1953–1968.* October House, 1968.

Riasanovsky, Nicholas V., *A History of Russia.* Oxford University Press, 1977.

St. George, George, and the Editors of Time-Life Books, *Soviet Deserts and Mountains* (The World's Wild Places series) Time-Life Books, 1974.

Schecter, Jerrold and Leona; and Evelind, Steven, Kate, Doveen and Barnet, *An American Family in Moscow.* Little, Brown, 1975.

Silianoff, Eugene, *The Russians.* Little, Brown, 1980.

Simis, Konstantin, *U.S.S.R.: The Corrupt Society.* Dent, 1982.

Smith, Hedrick, *The Russians.* Sphere Books, 1977.

Solzhenitsyn, Alexander I., *The Gulag Archipelago.* Collins/Harvill Press, 1974–78.

Stanislavsky, Constantin, *My Life in Art.* Eyre Methuen, 1980.

Tolstoy, Leo, *War and Peace.* Simon and Schuster, 1958.

Treadgold, Donald W., *Twentieth Century Russia.* Rand McNally, 1972.

Treml, Vladimir G., *Alcohol in the U.S.S.R., A Statistical Study.* Duke Press Policy Studies, 1982.

Troyat, Henri, *Pushkin.* Doubleday, 1970.

Ulam, Adam B.:
*The Bolsheviks.* Macmillan, 1965.
*Russia's Failed Revolutions: From the Decembrists to the Dissidents.* Weidenfeld & Nicolson, 1981.

Voinovich, Vladimir, *In Plain Russian.* Jonathan Cape, 1980.

Wädekin, Karl-Eugen:
*Agrarian Policies in Communist Europe.* The Hague: Allanheld, Osmun, 1982.
*The Private Sector in Soviet Agriculture.* University of California Press, 1973.

Wallace, Robert, and the Editors of Time-Life Books, *Rise of Russia* (Great Ages of Man series). Time-Life Books, 1967.

Wilson, Edmund, *To the Finland Station.* Fontana, 1970.

Yarmolinsky, Avrahm, *Two Centuries of Russian Verse.* Random House, 1966.

Yevtushenko, Yevgeny:
*Bratsk Station and Other New Poems.* Anchor, 1967.
*Yevtushenko's Reader.* Dutton, 1972.

## PERIODICALS

Crankshaw, Edward, "The Black Sheep of the Pokrovskoe." *New York Review of Books,* May 27, 1982.

Feifer, George:
"Russian Disorders." *Harper's,* Feb. 1981.
"Russian Winter." *Harper's,* Feb. 1982.

Greenfield, Marc, "Life Among the Russians." *New York Times Magazine,* Oct. 24, 1982.

Jordan, Robert Paul:
"The Proud Armenians," *National Geographic,* June 1978.
"Siberia's Empire Road, The River Ob." *National Geographic,* Feb. 1976.

Kraft, Joseph, "A Letter from Moscow." *New Yorker,* Jan. 31, 1983.

Lubin, Nancy, "Mullah and Commissar." *Geo,* June 1980.

Madison, Berenice, "The Problem That Won't Go Away." *Wilson Quarterly,* Autumn 1978.

Rythkeu, Yuri, "People of the Long Spring." *National Geographic,* Feb. 1983.

Simis, Konstantin, "Russia's Underground Millionaires." *Fortune,* June 29, 1981.

*Time:*
"Living Conveniently on the Left." June 23, 1980.
"OPEC Knuckles Under." Mar. 28, 1983.
"The Tough Search for Power." June 23, 1980.

Wädekin, Karl-Eugen, "Soviet Agriculture's Dependence on the West." *Foreign Affairs,* Spring 1982.

# INDEX

*Page numbers in italics refer to illustrations.*

## A

Afghanistan, 102, 103, 106, 151
Agriculture: arable land, 47–48; in Central Asia,
    73; and climate, *chart* 11, 48, 50; collective
    farms, *10–11*, 51, 53, *77*, 105, 148; farm workers,
    *52, 71, 77*; irrigation, 48, 50, 73; private
    enterprise, 50, 51, *53*, 148, 154; state farms and
    farming, *49*, 50–51, *50–51*, 105, 148;
    Transcaucasian produce, 70; under Stalin, 17,
    50, 102, 105. *See also* Animal husbandry; Crops
Akhmadulina, Bella, *see* Messerer
Akhmatova, Anna (poet), 128
Alexander I, Tsar, 101, 118
Alexander II, Tsar, 101, 103, 120
Alexander III, Tsar, 104
Alexis (Peter the Great's son), 97–98
Alma-Ata (Kazakhstan), 26, 54, 73
Alphabets, 67, 75; Cyrillic, 20
Altai region, fur hunter, *55*
Amalrik, Andrei (dissident writer), 53
Andropov, Yuri, 102, 150
Animal husbandry: cattle, *50–51*, 73, *77, 84*;
    collectivization, 73, 76; goats, 73, 80, *88–89*;
    horses, 73; reindeer, 53–54, 76, *82*; sheep, 73, *77*.
    *See also* Fur trade
Aral Sea, 48, 49, 73
Area of country, 16, 45
Armenia, *49*, 70, *map* 70, 71, 75, 137; Apostolic
    Church, *71, 78*; Christians, 67, 78, 79;
    earthquake, *103*; rock band, *129*
Army, *see* Military forces
Arts: censored and repressed, 117, 127–129;
    Faberge eggs, *120*; folk art (architectural), 54,
    *122–123*; icons, *121*; under *glasnost*, 117, 129;
    unions, 127–128. *See also* Ballet; Films and film-
    making; Music; Literature; Painting; Poets and
    poetry; Theatre
Avars, 91, 100
Azerbaijan, 70, *map* 70, 71–72, 75, 137, *155*;
    Muslims, 67, 78, 79

## B

Baikal, *see* Lake Baikal
Baikal-Amur Mainline (BAM), *58–59, 60–61*, 140
Baku, 16, 48, 70, *155*
Ballet, 57, *83*, 117, 126, 127, *127*; Bolshoi, 142
Baltic Coast, *44–45*; peoples, *map* 70
Batovrin, Sergei (dissident), *152*
Belorussia, 47, *48, 50–51, 53*, 69, 70, *map* 70, 75
Birth control, 23
Birth rate, 23; Asian, 73, *chart* 76; Muslim, 78
Black market, *see* Economy
Bloody Sunday (1905), 101, 103
Bolsheviks, 17, 101, 102, 104, 105, 139
*Boris Godunov* (opera), 118, 127
Borodin, Aleksandr (composer), 126–127
Brezhnev, Leonid (President), *102*, 150
Brodsky, Joseph (dissident poet), 128
Buffer states, *see* Communist satellite states
Bukhara (Uzbekistan), *79*

Buryat region, 54
Buryats (people), *map* 70, 75

## C

Cars: ownership, 14, 21, *21*, 148; production, *chart*
    14, *141–145*, 152, 154
Caspian Sea, 45, 48
Catherine II (the Great), Empress, 98–99, 101;
    crown, 98, *99*
Caucasus: irrigation, 48; long-lifers, 71–72, *72*;
    oil, 46; peoples, 70–72, *map* 70
Caucasus mountains, 45–46
Central Asia, 46, 72–74; birth rate, 73, *chart* 76;
    Muslims, 67; Volga Germans, 76
Chagall, Marc (painter), 79, 124
Chekhov, Anton (writer), 126
Chaptsov, Efim (painter), *125*
Chernenko, Konstantin, 102, 150
Chernobyl, 103
Chess, 28, *34*
Children, 30, 32, *33, 36, 66*; day-care, 32, 51, 142,
    *142*; "links", 32; and outdoor sounds, *32*;
    political organisations, 30; Young Pioneers, 30,
    *136*
Chukchi (people), *map* 70, 75–76
Cimmerians, 91, 100
Cinemas, 28, *143*. *See also* Films and film-making
Circus, *23*
Cities, 16
Civil War, white and Red armies (1918), *102*,
    104–105, *105, 125*
Climate, *chart* 11, 45, 48, 50
Coal, 46, *chart* 47, 53, 73
Cold War, 102, 106, 151
Committee for State Security (KGB), 102, 148,
    150
Communist Party, 17, 68, 102, 103, 105, 137, 138–
    139, 152; Five-Year Plans, 50, 105, 139–140,
    154; General Secretary, 138, 139; Plan, 139,
    147–148; privileges, 21, *138*, 139
Communist satellite states (buffer states), 102,
    103, 106, 137, 151
Consumer goods, 12, *12–13*, 19–20, 21, 25–26, 147,
    150; pet market, *22*
Cossacks, 54, 99, 101
Crimea, 47, 99, 100, 101; Tartars, 67, 76, 78
Crops, 48, 50, 51, 53, 69, 73
Czechoslovakia, 102, 106, *107*

## D

Dachas ("country villas"), 16, 29, *34–35*, 131, *135*,
    139
Dams, *see* Irrigation and dams
Decembrist Revolt (1825), 101, 103
Defence, *see* Military forces; Nuclear weapons
*Demokratizatsiya* (democratization), 19, 137
Dissidents, 53, 103, 128, 138, 148, *152*
Dnieper, River, 45, 91, 99
Dniester, River, 45
Don, River, 45
Dostoevsky, Fyodor (writer), 117, 120–123, 124
Dovzhenko, Alexander (film director), 29
Drink, *see* Food and drink
Duma (1905), 101, 103, 104

## E

Economy, 20, 21, 137, 139, *140*, 147, 150, 151–152,
    154–155; *fartsovshchiki* (black-market
    merchants), 148; secondary economy (black
    market), *21*, 23, 27, 70, 138, 148. *See also*
    Communist Party; Private enterprise
Education: schools, 17, 32, 33, 75; universities,
    32, 75, 150
Eisenstein, Sergei (film director), 29
El Lissitzky (painter), 124, *125*
Employment, *80–89, 141–145*; laziness, *140*;
    moonlighting, 25, 148
Environment: destruction of permafrost, *64*;
    pollution, 17; rivers and lakes polluted by
    industry, 48, 54–55; rivers reversed, 48, 49–50
Estonia, 28, 67, 103, 137; peoples, *map* 70
Ethnic groups, 32–33, 67–68, *map* 70, 75;
    deportations, 76, 78; under *glasnost*, 67, 69, 70,
    78–79, 137, *155*. *See also* names of peoples and
    countries
Evenks (people), 76

## F

Faberge, Carl (jeweller), *120*
Factories, 12, 140, *141–145*, 147, 150, 152, 154;
    "underground" factories, 138, 148
Films and film-making, 19, 28–29, 57, 117, 127,
    129
Five-Year Plans, *see* Communist Party
Food and drink: alcohol, *27*, 30; Azerbaijani, 72;
    consumption, 20; family meals, 23, *24*, 25;
    feasting, *94–95*; from factories, 143; Georgian,
    70–71; home-brewed drink, 30, 53; in Siberian
    temperatures, *56*, 57; sturgeon and caviare, *24*,
    48–49; subsidies and shortages, 12, 154, 155;
    Ukrainian bread, 69–70; Uzbek, 74, 75, *75*
Forestry and forests, 17, 46, 53
Fur trade, 53, 54, *55, 80*, 101
Fyodor (Ivan IV's son), 95, 101

## G

Geography, 45–46
Georgia, *66*, 67, 70–71, *map* 70, *72, 86–87*, 103, 137;
    annexed, 70, 101; Khevsur tribe, *90–91*
*Glasnost* (openness), 19, 20, 103, 137, 151, 152; the
    arts, 117; nationalism, 67, 69, 70; the press, 28;
    religion, 78, 79
Godunov, Boris, Tsar, 95, 101
Gogol, Nikolai (playwright, novelist), 119–120
Gorbachev, Mikhail, 102–103, 137–138, 150–152,
    154; anti-alcohol campaign, 30; reforms, 12,
    19, 129, 137, 151–152, 154–155; visits Pope, 78
Gorky, 21; factory, 143
Gromyko, Andrei (Foreign Minister), 150
Gross domestic product, 12
Gross national product, 146, 155

## H

Health care, 25, 139, 141, *142*
Hero projects, 58, 140
History: chronological summary, 100–103; tribal
    invasions, 91–92; origins of Russian state
    (10th–15th centuries), 92; tsars (15th–17th
    centuries), 92–93, 95–98; early Western

influences (17th–18th centuries), 96–97, 98; end of monarchy (19th and early 20th century), 103–104; communism, and Iron Curtain (20th century), 104–106

Housing, 20; Azerbaijan, 70; building techniques in permafrost regions, 56, *57*; countryside, *36*; factory-sponsored, 141, *142*; fireplaces, *134*; home-swapping, *22, 23*; intelligentsia family, 21–22; Irkutsk, 54; *izbi* (agricultural cottages), 51, *52, 53*; *khrushchobi*, 22; prefabricated, 16, *17*, 22; Stalinist era, 22; state farm workers, 51; subsidized, 21, 155; Ukrainian, 69; urban, 16, 34, *37*; *yarangi*, 75. *See also* Dachas

Hungary, 102, 151

Hydroelectricity, 47, 48, 70

**I**

Industry, 16, 17, 140, 150; Kirgizia, 73; Ukraine, 69; under Stalin, 102, 106, 140; Siberia, 54. *See also* Cars; Factories; Hydroelectricity; Minerals; Natural gas; Oil industry; Textile industry

Irkutsk (Siberia), 54, 55, *136*; village near, *56*

Iron ore, 17, 47, *chart 47*

Irrigation and dams, 47, 48–50; canal, 73; Siberian, 54, 55–56

Ivan I, Prince of Moscow, 100

Ivan III (the Great), 92, *100*

Ivan IV (the Terrible), 7, 93, *93*, 95, 100–101; feast, *94–95*; *oprichniki*, 95, *101*

**J**

Jews and Judaism, 67, 78, 79, *86*, 92

Justice system, 150

**K**

Kama, River, lorry factory, 140

Kandinsky, Vasily (painter), 124

Kara-Kum desert, 73, *74*

Kazakhs, *map* 70, 75, 79

Kazakhstan, 49, 50, 73, 80

Kerensky, Alexander, 102

KGB, *see* Committee for State Security

Khabarovsk (Siberia), prefabricated building, *17*

Kharkov, underground railway, 16

Khazars (people), 68, 91, 92, 100

Khrushchev, Nikita, 22, *102*, 139, 152

Kiev (Ukraine), 16, 47, 69, 92, 100; intelligentsia class lifestyle, 21–22

Kirgizia, *map* 70, 73

Kirgiz (people), *map* 70, 79

Kola Peninsula, 11

**L**

Lake Baikal, 54–55

Languages, 67

Latvia, 67, *map* 70, 137

Leisure, 28–30; *bania* (steam baths), 29–30; holidays, 29, 34, *40–41, 42*, 145; parks, *28*, 34, *42–43*; slides, *46*. *See also* Chess

Lena, River (Siberia), 48

Leningrad, 16, 21, 22, 47, *83*. *See also* St. Petersburg

Lenin, Vladimir (Ulianov), 45, 78, 97, 104, 105, 101, *102*

Lermontov, Mikhail (poet), 119

Literacy, 17, 28

Literature, 19, 28, 117–118, 119–124, 126, 127–129; Writers' Union, 128, 131

Lithuania, 67, 68, 101, 103, 137; peoples, *map* 70, 91

**M**

Malevich, Kazimir (painter), 124, 129

Marine Resources, fishing venture with US, *149*

Marriages, *31, 33*, 80, *112*; of convenience, 22

Marx, Karl, 138; Marxism, 104, 139, 154

Matiushin, Mikhail (musician, artist), 124, *125*

Mensheviks, 101

Meshketian Turks, 67

Messerer, Boris (artist), and Bella (n[130]e Akhmadulina, poet), lifestyle, *130–135*

Michurinsk, Lenin Factory near, 152, 154

Military forces, 17, 138; defence spending, 106, 146, 151; during World War I, 103; reduction of numbers under Gorbachev, 137, 151; Russian generals, 68; service, 33; technology, 146–147

Minerals, 45, 46, 47, 53, 55, 80

Minsk, factory, 143

Moldavia, 67, *map* 70, 137

Mongolians, 67, *map* 70

Moscow, 47, 68; Academy of Sciences, 140, 142; Art Theatre, 127; chessplayers, *34*; Children's World (toy shop), 19; dacha zone, 16, *34–35*; dance schools, *127*; Eastern European imports, 19; fishermen, *41*; GUM department store, *12–13*, 19; "hooligans", *25*; housing, 22, *37*; Ice Circus, *23*; Leninsky Komsomol Automobile Plant (AZLK), *141–145*; Lenin's tomb, 19, 33; Metro, 16; newlyweds, 33; newspapers, 127; origins, 92, *92*, 100; parks, 16, *42–43*; population, 16; Red Square, 19; residency permits, 22; St. Basil's Cathedral, *6–7*, 19, 93, 100; Sandunovsky baths, 29–30; sunshine hours, 44; Tartar demonstrations, 78; theatre, 97; university, 32–33; Western influences, 19; women, *18, 80–81*; Yiddish newspapers, 79

Music, 125, 126; Mighty Handful, 126, 127; rock bands, 19, 129, *129*

Muslims, 30, 67, 76, *chart 76*, 78–79, *79*

Mussorgsky, Modest (composer), 126, 127

**N**

Nabokov, Vladimir (novelist), quoted, 117

Napoleon Bonaparte, *101*, 103

Natural gas, 17, 46; pipeline, 46, *153*

Nenets (people), *map* 70, 76, *82*

Nevsky, Alexander, Prince of Novgorod, 100

Newspapers, 28, 70, 79, 127

Ngorno Karabakh, 70

Nicholas I, Tsar, 118

Nicholas II, Tsar, 101, 103, 104, 105; Faberge egg, *120*

Nijinsky, Waslaw (dancer), 117, 127

Northern Dvina, River, 49

Novgorod, 92, 95, 100, 101; icon, *121*

Novosibirsk (Siberia), 16; Akademgorodok, 140

Nuclear power, 47, 103, 146

Nuclear weapons, 102, 103, 106, 137, 151

**O**

Ob, River (Siberia), 48, 49

October Revolution (1917), 102, 104

Odessa (port), 11; rest home, 29

Oil industry, 17, 46, *chart 47*, 54, 55, 70

Oleg, Prince, *100*

Olympics, *8–9*

Onega, River, 48, 49

Orthodox Church, *see* Religion

**P**

Painting, 27, *124–125*, 127, *128*, 129

Pamir mountains, 46, 73

Pasternak, Boris (writer), 28, 117, 128–129

Peat, 46–47, *48*

Pechenegs (people), 91 Pechora, River, 48, 49

*Perestroika* (reconstruction), 12, 19, 20, 103, 137, 151, 152, 154

Permafrost, 55–56, *64–65*

Peter the Great, Tsar, 19, 95–98, *96*, 101, 117, *119*; axe, *101*

Piukhtitsy (Estonia), convents, *111*

Poets and poetry, 27, 117, 118–119, 127, 128, *131–132*, 152

Poland, 68, 91, 95, 101, 102, 106, 151

Politburo, 68, 138, 139

Pollution, *see* Environment

Population: Belorussians, 69; Central Asia, 73; Moscow, 16; Russians, 68; USSR, 19, 68, 70

Private enterprise, 12, *21*, 25, 137, 148, 152, 154–155; in agriculture, 50, 51, *53*, 148, 154

Pudovkin, Vsevolod (film director), 29

Pugachev (Cossack rebel), 99

Pushkin, Alexander (poet), 118–119, *118*

**Q**

Queues, 12, 19, 20, 26, *38*

**R**

Railways, *see* Baikal-Amur Mainline; Trans-Siberian Express

Rasputin, Grigory (monk), 103, *104*, 101

Red Army, 104, 105, 106; poster, *125*

Religion, 67; Armenian, *71, 78*; ethnic resurgence under *glasnost*, 78; icons, *121*; Orthodox Church, 78, 92, *108–115*. *See also* Jews and Judaism; Muslims

Rimsky-Korsakov, Nikolai (composer), 117, 126, 127

Rivers, *see* Environment; Irrigation and dams

Romanov dynasty, 95, 103, 117

Romanov, Mikhail, Tsar, 95, 101

Russians (people), *66*, 67–69, 70, *map* 70, 91; birth rate, 23, *chart 76*; in Central Asia, 72, 73; and other ethnic groups, 79

Russian Soviet Federated Socialist Republic (R.S.F.S.R.), 68

Russo-Japanese War (1905), 101, 103

Rytkheu, Yuri (novelist), 75

**S**

St. Petersburg, *96*, 97, 98, 99, 101, *119*, 127; Decembrist Revolt, 101, 103. *See also* Leningrad

Sakharov, Andrei (physicist), 146

Samarkand, 74

Sarmatians, 91, 100

Science and technology, 140, 146. *See also* Space exploration

Scythians, 91, 100, *100*

Serfdom, 98–99, 101, *101*, 103, 124

Severnaya Zemlya (island), 45

Shops and shopping, 12, 23, 25, 26, 34, *38–39*, *138*, *143*; abacuses, *39*, 146; *beriozki*, *138*, 148. *See also* Queues

Siberia: alcohol, 30; Arctic peoples, 75–76; collective farm, *10–11*; Cossacks, 101; decorated window frames, *122–123*; diamonds, 47; economic development, 33, 53–54, 58; furs, *55*, *80*; jobs, *88–89*; living in cold and frost, 55–57, *56*, *57*, *62–65*; long rouble, 57; natural gas pipeline, *153*; oil, 46; as place of banishment, 53, 95; receives deportees, 76, 78; taiga, 46, 54; transport, 54, *58–59*, *60–61*

Slavs, *map* 70, 91, 92; as Russians, 91; Slavic peoples, 68, 91, 100

Sochi, health spas, 29, *40–41*, *86–87*

Social Democratic Party, 101

Solzhenitsyn, Alexander (writer), 28, 117, 120

Space exploration, 17, 102, 106, 137, 140, 146, *146*

Sport, *8–9*; facilities, 29, *144*

Stalin, Joseph, 17, 46, 70, *102*, 105–106; anti-Semitism, 79; and the arts, 117, 124, 127–128; Baltic States, 67; Five-Year Plans, 50, 105, 139–140; Great Purge, 102, 105; justice system, 150; and Muslims, 78

Stravinsky, Igor (composer), 117, 127

Subsidies, 21, 154, 155

Supreme Soviet, elections, 138–139

Suzdal: church service, *114–115*; monastery, *42*

**T**

Tadzhikistan, 73

Tadzhiks (people), 28, *map* 70, 73

Taiga, 46, 53

Tajiks (people), 79

Tamm, Igor (physicist), 146

Tartars (people), 67, 68, 70, *map* 70, 76, 78, 91, 92, 93, 100

Tashkent, 16, 74, 80, *88*

Tbilisi, underground railway 16

Tchaikovsky, Pyotr (composer), 117, 126, 127

Telephones: kiosks, *29*; ownership, 21

Television, 19, *26*, 28, 57; ownership, 12, 21

Textile industry, 73, 80

Theatre, 19, 57, 79, 127, 129, 143, *145*

Togliatti, factory, 143

Tolstoy, Leo (writer), *116*, 117, 123–124

Transport: buses, 16; on ice, 55; rivers, 48; roads, 73, Lenin Prospekt, *14–15*; Siberia, 54; underground railways, 16, 74. *See also* Baikal-Amur Mainline; Cars; Trans-Siberian Railway

Trans-Siberian Railway, 45, 54, *58–59*, 140

Trotsky, Leon, *102*, 105

Tundra, 11, 46

Turgenev, Ivan (writer), 124, 126

Turkmenistan, 50, 73

Turkomen (people), *map* 70, *74*

**U**

Ukraine and Ukrainians, 28, 47, 68, 69–70, *map* 70, 75, *84*, *85*, 101

Ulan Ude (city), 54

Urals, arable land, 47

Urbanization, 16–17; urbanites, 21

USSR, 67; established, 102

Uzbekistan, 49, 74; Tartar deportees, 76, 78

Uzbeks (people), 67, *67*, *map* 70, *73*, 74–75, *75*, 79

**V**

Varangians (people), 91–92, 100

Vehicle production, lorry factory, 140. *See also* Cars

Veprintsev, Boris (biophysicist), *32*

Vladimir, ruler of Kiev, 92, 100

Volga, River, 45, 48, 49; Volgograd dam, 47, 48

Volga region, deportation of Germans, 76

**W**

Walrus Club, *68–69*

Women: birth control, 23; childcare, *142*; lifestyle, 27–28; role in society, 26–27; in the workforce, 26–27, 51, *61*, *80–81*

World War I, 101, 103

World War II, 16, 102, 106, 108; deportations, 76, 78

**Y**

Yakutia, 80

Yakutsk (Siberia), 54, 56

Yakuts (people), *60–61*, 67, *map* 70, 75, 76

Yaroslav the Wise, 100

Yenisei, River (Siberia), 48

Yerevan, underground railway, 16

Yevtushenko, Yevgeny (poet), 91, 128

**Z**

Zagorsk, churches, *108*

Zakharina-Romanov, Anastasia (wife of Ivan IV), 93, 95, 100, 101

Colour separations by Scan Studios, Ltd., Dublin, Ireland

Typesetting by Tradespools Ltd., Somerset, England

Printed in Spain by Artes Graficas Toledo S.A.